RESOURCING MEDIA IN THE FRAMEWORK
FOR TEACHING ENGLISH

MEDIASCRIPTS

Scripts edited by Simon Page and Mark Warner

Activities written by Jonathan Morgan

Inspiring generations

Heinemann Educational Publishers
Halley Court, Jordan Hill, Oxford OX2 8EJ
Part of Harcourt Education

Heinemann is the registered trademark of
Harcourt Education Limited

Selection, introductions and activities © Jonathan Morgan, Simon Page,
Mark Warner, 2004

First published 2004

09 08 07 06 05 04
10 9 8 7 6 5 4 3 2 1

British Library Cataloguing in Publication Data is available
from the British Library on request.

ISBN 0 435 23334 3

Typeset by 🗦 Tek-Art, Croydon, Surrey

Printed in the United Kingdom by Clays Ltd

Cover design by mcdesign ltd

Tel: 01865 888058 www.heinemann.co.uk

Acknowledgements

Every effort has been made to contact copyright holders of material reproduced in this book. Any omissions will be rectified in subsequent printings if notice is given to the publishers.

Extract from *War of the Worlds* radio script, re-broadcast from the Mercury Theatre, July 1938. Written by Howard Koch. Copyright © 1940 Princeton University; copyright renewed 1967; copyright assigned to Howard Koch, 1969; this excerpt licensed to Heinemann Educational by Anne Koch for herself and other successors to Howard Koch; Extracts from BBC Radio 5 Live Fi Glover phone-in, 25th February 2003. Reproduced by permission of the BBC; Extract from *Coronation Street*, Scene 9, episode 5523. Written by Daran Little. Reprinted with the kind permission of the licensing dept of Granada Enterprises; Extract from an episode of *Grange Hill*, 19th March 2003. Written by Matthew Evans, directed by Chris Corcoran. Reprinted with permission of Phil Redmond and Grange Hill Productions Ltd; Extract from *House of Dracula* edited by Philip Riley, published by MagicImage Filmbooks. Reprinted by permission of Universal Studios, USA; Extract from *Wallace & Gromit – A Close Shave* by Nick Park. Copyright © Aardman/W&G Ltd and BBC Worldwide 1995. Reprinted with the kind permission of Aardman; Extract from *North by Northwest* by Ernest Lehman, published by Faber and Faber Ltd. Reprinted with permission of Faber and Faber Ltd; Extract from football commentary on Radio 5 Live – Glasgow Rangers versus Manchester United, Wednesday 22nd October 2003. Reprinted by permission of the BBC; Extract from an interview with James King, film critic, and Will Smith on Sarah Cox's Breakfast Show, 29th July 2002 on BBC Radio One UK. Permission granted by BBC; Extract from the script of *Only Fools and Horses* BBC Comic Relief Special by John Sullivan. Reprinted by permission of Comic Relief; Extract from the script of 'We Haven't Met' by Stephen Fry and Hugh Laurie from *A Bit of Fry and Laurie*. Reprinted by permission of Hamilton Hodell, on behalf of the authors; Extract from *KES: A Kestrel for a Knave* by Barry Hines. Copyright © Barry Hines, 1968. First published by Michael Joseph. Reproduced by permission of The Agency (London) Ltd, 24 Pottery Lane, London W11 4LZ. Fax: 0207 727 9037. All rights reserved. Extract from *The Full Monty* by Simon Beaufoy, published by Screenpress Books, 1997. Reprinted by permission of Screenpress Books; Extract from *The Hitchhikers' Guide to the Galaxy* by Douglas Adams, broadcast on BBC Radio 4, on 15th March 1978. Reprinted by permission of Ed Victor Ltd on behalf of the author; Extract from *FX* by Roger McGough, written for Radio Four, *Thirty Minute Theatre*. Copyright © 1989 Roger McGough. Reprinted by permission of PFD on behalf of Roger McGough; Extract from *Men Behaving Badly* by Simon Nye, published by Hodder Headline. Copyright © Simon Nye. Reprinted by permission of the Rod Hall Agency on behalf of the author; Extract from *The Complete Fawlty Towers* by John Cleese and Connie Booth. Copyright © John Cleese, Connie Booth, Waterfall Production Ltd 1977, 1979, 1988. First published by Methuen in 1988. Reprinted by permission of David Wilkinson Associates Ltd on behalf of the authors; Extract from *Secrets and Lies* by Mike Leigh, published by Faber and Faber Ltd. Reprinted by permission of Faber and Faber Ltd.

With the kind permission of the copyright holders, the following scripts have not been reproduced in their original form as any language that may be deemed offensive has been removed:

Extract from 'Kevin the Teenager' by Harry Enfield and Paul Whitehouse. Copyright © Harry Enfield, Paul Whitehouse and Charlie Higson. Reprinted by permission of Alexandra Cann Representation on behalf of Paul Whitehouse and Charlie Higson, and PBJ Management on behalf of Harry Enfield; Extract from 'Blackadder Goes Forth' from *Blackadder: The Whole Damn Dynasty* by Richard Curtis. Copyright © Richard Curtis. Reprinted by permission of PFD on behalf of Richard Curtis; Extract from *East is East* by Ayub Khan-Din. Copyright © Ayub Khan-Din, 1999. First published by FilmFour Books. Reproduced by permission of The Agency (London) Ltd, 24 Pottery Lane, London W11 4LZ. Fax: 0207 727 9037. All rights reserved; Extract from *The Royle Family* by Caroline Aherne, Craig Cash and Carmel Morgan, Series 2, Episode 7, published by Granada Media 2000. Reprinted by permission of P. McIntyre, on behalf of the authors; Extract from *Fever Pitch: The Screenplay* by Nick Hornby (Victor Gollancz 1992). Copyright © Nick Hornby, 1992. Reprinted by permission of Penguin Books UK, and PFD on behalf of the author; Extract from *Educating Rita* by Willy Russell, published by Methuen. Reprinted by permission of Methuen Publishing Ltd.

Contents

Section F: Conflict in Childhood

YEAR 9
Section G: What on Earth?

Section H: People Behaving Badly

Section I: Passion Fruits

Section J: Comparison Activities

Key

Radio

Television

Film

Introduction

Mediascripts provides a comprehensive collection of high-quality scripts for English at Key Stage 3. The texts and accompanying activities specifically target the objectives of the *Framework for Teaching English* for Year 7 to Year 9.

Extracts from radio, film and television scripts are immediately accessible and highly entertaining for young people. The diverse sources included here range from the popular and contemporary to those from less familiar cultural and historical contexts. All the texts included have been selected because of their potential for stimulating a genuine interest in language as a means of communication.

Mediascripts has ten chapters divided into radio, film and television. Each genre has one dedicated chapter for each of the three year groups at Key Stage 3. The chapters include differentiated activities, which are clearly linked to the Framework objectives. There is an objective linking grid at the back of the book to direct you to the appropriate page of activities. This will help ensure maximum coverage of the objectives and aid teachers with their Key Stage 3 planning.

As an extra dimension the chapters are also arranged according to theme, allowing for interesting comparisons within chapters. The final chapter prompts comparisons across the chapters, the themes and the three media.

Opportunities are provided for a range of activities; from role play, script writing, film analysis and drama to developing students' understanding of character, dramatic devices, language and action. Students will feel well-equipped to tackle the challenging demands of understanding and accessing the overwhelming and influential media of today.

Section A: Get Real!

A1: The War of the Worlds

Introduction

This script is a radio play based on the novel of the same name by H.G. Wells.

It is about a Martian invasion of Earth. When it was broadcast on the radio by Orson Welles from the Mercury Theatre in America in 1938, many people thought it was a real news bulletin. As a result, there was mass panic all over the country. One of the main reasons why people were fooled was because the broadcast used the conventions of radio news so convincingly. It is a good example of a piece of fiction being mistaken for something that is factual.

This extract begins a few minutes into the broadcast.

Number of parts: 7
Parts in order of appearance:

Announcer three
Announcer two
Carl Phillips, commentator
Professor Richard Pierson
Policeman
Mr Wilmuth
Voices

War of the Worlds

ANNOUNCER THREE   Good evening, ladies and gentlemen. From the Meridian Room in the Park Plaza in New York City, we bring you the music of Ramon Raquello and his orchestra. With a touch of the Spanish. Ramon Raquello leads off with 'La Cumparsita'.

Piece starts playing.

ANNOUNCER TWO   Ladies and gentlemen, we interrupt our programme of dance music to bring you a special bulletin from the Intercontinental Radio News. At twenty minutes before eight, central time, Professor Farrell of the Mount Jennings Observatory, Chicago, Illinois, reports observing several explosions of incandescent gas, occurring at regular intervals on the planet Mars. The spectroscope indicates the gas to be hydrogen and moving towards the Earth with enormous velocity. Professor Pierson of the Observatory at Princeton confirms Farrell's observation, and describes the phenomenon as (quote) like a jet of blue flame shot from a gun (unquote). We now return you to the music of Ramon Raquello, playing for you in the Meridian Room of the Park Plaza Hotel, situated in downtown New York.

Music plays for a few moments until piece ends . . . Sound of applause.

ANNOUNCER THREE   Now a tune that never loses favour, the ever-popular 'Star Dust'. Ramon Raquello and his orchestra . . .

Music.

ANNOUNCER TWO   Ladies and gentlemen, following on the news given in our bulletin a moment ago, the Government Meteorological Bureau has requested the large observatories of the country to keep an astronomical watch on any further disturbances occurring on the planet Mars. Due to the unusual nature of this occurrence, we have arranged an interview with noted astronomer, Professor Pierson, who will give us his views on the event. In a few moments we will take you to the Princeton Observatory at Princeton, New Jersey. We return you until then to the music of Ramon Raquello and his orchestra.

Music.

ANNOUNCER TWO   We are now ready to take you to the Princeton Observatory at Princeton where Carl Phillips, our commentator, will interview Professor Richard Pierson, famous astronomer. We take you now to Princeton, New Jersey.

*Echo chamber. **FX**: Tick-Tock Sound.*

PHILLIPS   Good evening, ladies and gentlemen. This is Carl Phillips, speaking to you from the observatory at Princeton. I am standing in a large semi-circular room, pitch black except for an oblong split in the ceiling. Through this opening I can see a sprinkling of stars that cast a kind of frosty glow over the intricate mechanism of the huge telescope. The ticking sound you hear is the vibration of clockwork. Professor Pierson stands directly above me on a small platform, peering through a giant lens.

I ask you to be patient, ladies and gentlemen, during any delay that may arise during our interview. Besides his ceaseless watch of the heavens, Professor Pierson may be interrupted by telephone or other communications. During this period he is in constant touch with the astronomical centres of the world . . . Professor, may I begin our questions?

PIERSON   At any time, Mr Phillips.

PHILLIPS   Professor, would you please tell our radio audience exactly what you see as you observe the planet Mars through your telescope?

PIERSON   Nothing unusual at the moment, Mr. Phillips. A red disk swimming in a blue sea. Transverse stripes across the disk. Quite distinct now because Mars happens to be the point nearest to the Earth . . . in opposition, as we call it.

PHILLIPS   In your opinion, what do these transverse stripes signify, Professor Pierson?

PIERSON   Not canals, I can assure you Mr Phillips, although that's the popular conjecture of those who imagine Mars to be inhabited. From a scientific viewpoint the stripes are merely the result of atmospheric conditions peculiar to the planet.

PHILLIPS   Then you're quite convinced as a scientist that living intelligence as we know it does not exist on Mars?

PIERSON   I'd say the chances are a thousand to one.

PHILLIPS   And yet how do you account for those gas eruptions occurring on the surface of the planet at regular intervals?

PIERSON   Mr Phillips, I cannot account for it.

PHILLIPS	By the way, Professor, for the benefit of our listeners, how far is Mars from Earth?
PIERSON	Approximately forty million miles.
PHILLIPS	Well that seems a safe enough distance. *(Off mike)* Thank you.

Pause.

PHILLIPS	Just a moment ladies and gentlemen, someone has just handed Professor Pierson a message. While he reads it, let me remind you that we are speaking from the observatory in Princeton, New Jersey, where we are interviewing the world-famous astronomer, Professor Pierson . . . One moment, please. Professor, may I read the message to the listening audience?
PIERSON	Certainly, Mr Phillips.
PHILLIPS	Ladies and gentlemen, I shall read you a wire addressed to Professor Pierson from Dr Gray of the National History Museum, New York. '9.15 P.M. Eastern Standard Time. Seismograph registered shock of almost earthquake intensity occurring within a radius of twenty miles of Princeton. Please investigate. Signed, Lloyd Gray, Chief of Astronomical Division' . . . Professor Pierson, could this occurrence possibly have something to do with the disturbances observed on the planet Mars?
PIERSON	Hardly, Mr Phillips. This is probably a meteorite of unusual size and its arrival at this particular time is merely a coincidence. However, we shall conduct a search as soon as daylight permits.

PHILLIPS Thank you, Professor. Ladies and gentlemen, for the past ten minutes we've been speaking to you from the observatory at Princeton, bringing you a special interview with Professor Pierson, noted astronomer. This is Carl Phillips speaking. We are returning you now to our New York studio.

Fade in piano playing.

ANNOUNCER TWO Ladies and gentlemen, here is the latest bulletin from the Intercontinental Radio News. Toronto, Canada: Professor Morse of McGill University reports observing a total of three explosions on the planet Mars, between the hours of 7:45 P.M. and 9:20 P.M., Eastern Standard Time. This confirms earlier reports received from American observatories. Now, nearer home, comes a special announcement from Trenton, New Jersey. It is reported that at 8:50 P.M. a huge, flaming object, believed to be a meteorite, fell on a farm in the neighbourhood of Grovers Mill, New Jersey, twenty-two miles from Trenton.

The flash in the sky was visible within a radius of several hundred miles and the noise impact was heard as far north as Elizabeth.

We have dispatched a special mobile unit to the scene, and will have our commentator, Carl Phillips, give you a word description as soon as he can each there from Princeton. In the meantime, we take you to the Hotel Martinet in Brooklyn, where Bobby Millette and his orchestra are offering a programme of dance music.

Swing band for twenty seconds . . . then cut.

ANNOUNCER TWO We now take you to Grovers Mill, New Jersey.

Crowd noises . . . Police sirens.

PHILLIPS Ladies and gentlemen, this is Carl Phillips again, at the Wilmuth farm, Grovers Mill, New Jersey. Professor Pierson and myself made the eleven miles from Princeton in ten minutes. Well, I . . . I hardly know where to begin, to paint for you a word picture of the strange scene before my eyes, like something out of a modern 'Arabian Nights'. Well I just got here. I haven't had a chance to look around yet. I guess that's it. Yes, I guess that's the . . . thing, directly in front of me, half buried in a vast pit. Must have struck with terrific force. The ground is covered with splinters of a tree it must have struck on its way down. What can I see of the . . . object itself doesn't look very much like a meteor, at least not the meteors I've seen. It looks more like a huge cylinder. It has a diameter of . . . what would you say, Professor Pierson?

PIERSON *(off mike)* What's that?

PHILLIPS What would you say . . . what is the diameter?

PIERSON About thirty yards.

PHILLIPS About thirty yards . . . the metal on the sheath is . . . well, I've never seen anything like it. The colour is sort of yellowish-white. Curious spectators now are pressing close to the object in spite of the efforts of the police to keep them back. They're getting in front of my line of vision. Would you mind standing to one side, please?

POLICEMAN	One side, there, one side.
PHILLIPS	While the policemen are pushing the crowd back, here's Mr Wilmuth, owner of the farm here. He may have some interesting facts to add . . . Mr Wilmuth, would you please tell the radio audience as much as you remember of this rather unusual visitor that dropped in your backyard? Step closer, please. Ladies and gentlemen, this is Mr Wilmuth.
WILMUTH	Well I was listenin' to the radio.
PHILLIPS	Closer and louder please.
WILMUTH	Pardon me?!
PHILLIPS	Louder, please, and closer.
WILMUTH	Yes, sir – I was listening to the radio and kinda drowsin'. That Professor fellow was talkin' about Mars, so I was half dozin' and half . . .
PHILLIPS	Yes, yes Mr Wilmuth. Then what happened?
WILMUTH	As I was sayin', I was listenin' to the radio kinda halfways . . .
PHILLIPS	Yes, Mr Wilmuth, and then you saw something?
WILMUTH	Not first off. I heard something.
PHILLIPS	And what did you hear?
WILMUTH	A hissing sound. Like this: SSSSSSS . . . kinda like a fourt' of July rocket.
PHILLIPS	Yes, then what?
WILMUTH	Turned my head out the window and would have swore I was to sleep and dreamin'.
PHILLIPS	Then what?
WILMUTH	I seen a kinda greenish streak and then zingo! Somethin' smacked the ground. Knocked me clear out of my chair!

PHILLIPS   Well, were you frightened, Mr Wilmuth?

WILMUTH   Well, I – I ain't quite sure. I reckon I – I was kinda riled.

PHILLIPS   Thank you, Mr Wilmuth. Thank you.

WILMUTH   You want me to tell you some more?

PHILLIPS   No . . . that's quite alright, that's plenty.

PHILLIPS   Ladies and gentlemen, you've just heard Mr Wilmuth, owner of the farm where this thing has fallen. I wish I could convey the atmosphere . . . the background of this . . . fantastic scene. Hundreds of cars are parked in a field in back of us. Police are trying to rope off the roadway leading to the farm. But it's no use. They're breaking right through. Cars' headlights throw an enormous spot on the pit where the object's half buried. Some of the more daring souls are now venturing near the edge. Their silhouettes stand out against the metal sheen.

Faint humming sound.

One man wants to touch the thing . . . he's having an argument with a policeman. The policeman wins . . . Now, ladies and gentlemen, there's something I haven't mentioned in all this excitement, but now it's becoming more distinct. Perhaps you've caught it already on your radio. Listen:

Long pause.

Do you hear it? It's a curious humming sound that seems to come from inside the object. I'll move the microphone nearer. *(Pause)* Now we're not more than twenty-five feet away. Can you hear it now? Oh, Professor Pierson!

PIERSON Yes, Mr Phillips?

PHILLIPS Can you tell us the meaning of that scraping noise inside the thing?

PIERSON Possibly the unequal cooling of its surface.

PHILLIPS I see, do you still think it's a meteor, Professor?

PIERSON I don't know what to think. The metal casing is definitely extraterrestrial . . . not found on this Earth. Friction with the Earth's atmosphere usually tears holes in a meteorite. This thing is smooth and as you can see, of cylindrical shape.

PHILLIPS Just a minute! Something's happening! Ladies and gentlemen, this is terrific! The end of the thing is beginning to flake off! The top is beginning to rotate like a screw! The thing must be hollow!

VOICES She's movin'! Look, the darn thing's unscrewing! Keep back there! Keep back, I tell you! Maybe there's men in it trying to escape! It's red hot, they'll burn to a cinder! Keep back there. Keep those idiots back!

Suddenly the clanking sound of a huge piece of falling metal.

VOICES She's off! The top's loose! Look out there! Stand back!

PHILLIPS Ladies and gentlemen, this is the most terrifying thing I have ever witnessed . . . Wait a minute! Someone's crawling out of the hollow top. Someone or . . . something. I can see peering out of that black hole two luminous disks . . . are they eyes? It might be a face. It might be . . .

Shout of awe from the crowd.

Activities: War of the Worlds

As this script was written to be broadcast live, it is in the present tense. This has the effect of making the piece seem more realistic, immediate and intense for the listeners. This differs from recount writing (e.g. diary entry, report), which is in the past tense and has no immediate 'live' impact on the reader.

1 Rewrite the section of Phillips' speech from 'I wish I could convey the atmosphere' to 'It might be a face. It might be . . .' into a diary entry. Make the piece sound dramatic and exciting. You will find an example of how to change the script from present to past below.

Original live radio script Present tense	Diary entry (Recount) Past tense
Yes, I guess that's the . . . thing, directly in front of me, half buried in a vast pit. Must have struck with terrific force. The ground is covered with splinters of a tree it must have struck on its way down. What I can see of the . . . object itself doesn't look very much like a meteor, at least not the meteors I've seen. It looks more like a huge cylinder.	Then I <u>saw</u> the thing. It <u>was</u> half buried in a vast pit that <u>was</u> directly in front of me. I <u>could tell</u> that it <u>must have struck</u> with a terrible force. The ground <u>was</u> covered with tree splinters, which it <u>had struck</u> on its way down. It <u>didn't look</u> much like any meteors that I <u>have seen</u>. It <u>had</u> a diameter of about thirty yards. It <u>looked</u> more like a huge cylinder.

2   In the *War of the Worlds* script, there are many examples of the
following conventions of live news reporting:

- pauses
- repetition
- varied use of speech and sound effects.

In the table below there is an example to show where these
conventions are used and what effect these techniques have on
the listening audience. Using this as a guide, find one more
example for each convention, and explain its effect.

Conventions of live news reporting	Evidence	How this helps to convince the audience that the sighting is real
Pauses	What I can see of the . . . object	This helps to create the impression that the reporter is seeing the action as the listeners are hearing it. The pause creates a dramatic tension and sense of anticipation for the listener.
Repetition	Well, I – I ain't quite sure. I reckon I – I was kinda riled.	This helps the listener to empathise with the reporter and believe in his seeming sense of panic and fear which repetition often suggests.
Varied use of speech and sound effects	A hissing sound. Like this: SSSSSSS . . . kinda like a fourt' of July rocket.	

3 This radio broadcast managed to convince the listeners that the sighting was real. We have looked at the techniques used to make the report so convincing. However, the way that this report is delivered is even more important. In pairs, choose a section from Phillips' description of the sighting and practise reading this out loud. Remember to consider the following:

- dramatic pauses
- changes in tone
- intonation (emphasising key words)
- variation in volume
- use of repetition.

A2: Radio Five Live Phone-in

Introduction

Fi Glover presented a live morning phone-in show on BBC Radio Five Live. The programme slot is topical and therefore its content is shaped by the affairs of the day.

The following extract is from a programme broadcast in February 2003. At that time, ITV's *Coronation Street* was exciting audiences and tabloid newspaper editors with a storyline involving a serial killer. The topic for discussion is television soap operas and their effects on viewers.

Fi Glover's guest is *The Independent* newspaper's TV critic, James Rampton. Mike and Salim have rung in to the show to join in the discussion; Gareth is a TV executive from Granada Television. As you read through the extract, notice how the presenter manages to develop the discussion objectively so that the different views are expressed fairly.

Number of speakers: 5
Speakers in order of appearance:

Fi Glover
James Rampton
Mike
Gareth
Salim

Radio Five Live Phone-in

25th February 2003 9–9.30am

FI   We're talking about soaps this morning. Whether or not they're good for us. It's twenty minutes past nine. James Rampton replaces Steve Murphy. It's like a soap this morning, this programme in itself, James. It's almost like a shower scene. It was just a dream that we had Steve with us.

JAMES   Hello, I'm Bobby Ewing.

FI   Yes. You certainly are. Let me look at your webbed feet. You are the Independent's television critic. Do you therefore come to the idea of soaps with, I don't know, a slightly more broadsheet and therefore patronising attitude?

JAMES   Well, I hope not. I think there is a danger that broadsheet critics can seem quite snobbish about the soaps and I think that is something to be avoided because we've got to accept that they really do perform a function. I caught the end of the last discussion and I know there was a caller saying that he doesn't believe they educate people at all. But I think they do have a function in that they can raise awareness. I remember after the famous revelation of Mark Fowler having HIV. Aids help-lines said they were inundated with calls. They can bring people to an understanding about issues that they probably would never have considered otherwise, and it's because we sympathise with the characters. They can reach people in a way that, say, a worthy documentary about HIV, never could, because we feel very passionately about the characters. We're drawn into their lives and their plights. They touch us all in a way that some conventional programmes don't.

FI   It's a very British thing as well, James, isn't it? It's a very British thing. We do watch more soaps than any other country, and I wonder why that is. I mean, do you think ours are just better?

JAMES Well, it's one of the biggest clichés in the world, up there with comedy is the new rock 'n roll, to say that we have the best television in the world but we send *Archers* producers to Kazakhstan and to Angola to teach them how to make soaps because we do it very well. Oh God, I'm on real cliché alert here, but people have always said that Dickens was the first great soap writer. He wrote in weekly instalments. His novels appeared every week and people would be queuing up at the newsagents to buy them. I think we have a great tradition of storytelling. We love to hear about other people's lives and get wrapped up in them and I think soaps are carrying on in that tradition.

FI Let's hear from Mike who's in, is it Bungay, Mike?

MIKE Near Bungay. Harleston.

FI Right. Now, you've got kids.

MIKE I have.

FI Yes, do they watch the soaps?

MIKE Well, the older ones are grown up and the younger one is thirteen and she certainly has when I'm not looking. But, certainly, my concern is for those kids that are, sort of, under twelve who are exposed to this at half-past seven at night. It may be fine for adults to get all their issues out and understand them but you need a certain level of experience of life and understanding in order to see the context in which these issues are being played out. And we have many vulnerable young people in this country who are sitting there at half-past seven at night soaking this all up believing this is how adults behave. This is how you are when you're an adult. This is what you do. It's awful.

FI   Yes. It's a good point Gareth, isn't it? I mean it is very adult stuff. If we just move away from *Coronation Street*. On *EastEnders* last night, there's a plotline about Laura who's having somebody else's baby but they're all still involved in each other's families. You've got Dot and Jim breaking up. You've got families moving away, you know it's all about the darker side of life and **infidelity** comes up time and time again, which is possibly not the message you want to send to your kids about relationships.

GARETH   Yeah. I think first and foremost it's important that young kids, who I do accept can be more vulnerable, should be taught that this is a story, first and foremost. It's a fictional story. It does reflect life. These things can happen within life but by no means in one street or in one square would all these things happen. But I also think that the parents do have a responsibility that if they feel their child might be affected by something they've seen on a soap then hopefully that will lead to a discussion between parent and child.

MIKE   That is a complete cop out. On the basis of getting money, because you want the programme on at half-past seven. If you put it on at half-past nine, ten o'clock, you could have the same effect and value to the adult and you wouldn't necessarily be exposing vulnerable children whose, many of whose parents don't sit with them and watch it, don't explain anything. They're the people who we need to be concerned about.

GARETH   Well, what I would say to you Mike is that we have very stringent guidelines on *Coronation Street* and we are, we do consider ourself to be a family show. However, we are shown in the evening at seven-thirty.

MIKE   Well, you have a very odd idea about what families are about then, that's all I can say.

GARETH Well, we have a compliance department within Granada and we have very strict ITC rules and we feel very confident at *Coronation Street* that what we produce is a family drama and if you disagree with that, well that's fine, but of course, you know, we're offering an entertainment programme for our viewers and by no means we're forcing anyone to watch. And, of course, the viewer does always have the option of switching off if they find something they don't like.

MIKE Yes, but that's talking about adults. We're not talking about the kids. All the time he relates it to the adults. You don't actually look at the kids' perspective.

FI Mike. Have *you* had to explain any particular storylines or episodes to your thirteen year old.

MIKE Yes. On occasions when she's watched it and she's said about certain things then yes I will explain it. But I don't watch it. I hate the things. They're a complete, you know, something that some people love, some people hate but I wouldn't watch it. I hear the effect it has on teenagers. I hear the effect it has on other young people. They grow up with a warped sense of what adulthood is like.

FI Mike. Thank you for that. Gareth, we're going to hang the phone up on you and dial you again because we've got a bit of cut out on the line at the moment.

GARETH Oh okay.

FI So I don't want you to think that we're being rude, but go on someone, slam the phone down on him. Salim is in Woking, Mark is in Eversholt, and Geoff's in Southampton. Salim, good morning.

SALIM Hi. Good morning. How are you?

FI Yes. I'm very well. And you've got a very interesting point to make because you don't have a TV any more do you?

SALIM Yeah. We got rid of the TV two years ago and I must say it's done a tremendous amount of difference to the quality of our lives. My son was only five at the time. We involved him in the decision. I know one might argue that he's too young to be involved in the decision-making process but I think, I can tell you this much, you will be surprised how much these children can understand and looking back now I can only say that our family has benefited. I mean, I have some sympathy for the previous caller, I mean, what I would advise him is to try without TV for a couple of weeks and see what difference it makes to his life.

FI What did you do last night with your family then, Salim?

SALIM I did some homework with my kid. I played with him and I really sat down and spoke to my wife, which I don't do because I'm at work most of the time and you really forget how to spend time with your family if you are watching TV most of the time. Mind you, when I used to watch TV I used to love the soaps. Everybody loves the soaps. But I think, you know, overall that it does more harm than good.

FI Yes, your five year old. Does he not get left out of conversations? I suppose he is a little bit young but I mean I would imagine that a lot of his friends do, kind of, regurgitate the television characters and the cartoons and things like that.

SALIM I mean, yeah. I mean, that is a very strong argument and a lot of people did argue with us when I proposed this new change in our life but I went back to my own life. I grew up in India and I grew up without a TV and, believe me, I mean, I'm well informed. I'm a very knowledgeable person. I'm a doctor. I don't think you lose out if the TV's not there. I mean, there are other things to educate your children.

FI Sure. Do you find *yourself* getting left out of conversations though, at work, Salim? I mean is, you know, are there water cooler moments where you think I have got no idea who, I don't know, Homer Simpson is?

SALIM Not at all. I'll tell you why. Because I listen to your programme.

FI Oh right. So you can pick up the **detritus** of modern culture by listening to Five Live?

SALIM Of course. There was actually a study about newsworthy items, about news programmes in general and they found out that, you know, the newsworthy items are only, you know, five minutes worth. So you can catch up with it on the news on the radio. You don't really need to watch the telly, for example.

FI Yes. Can we put that in a trail? Cos, that's a lovely way to promote Five Live. Salim, it's nice to talk to you. Thank you very much indeed.

Activities: Radio Five Live Phone-in

In the opening section Fi and James refer to a famous shower scene from *Dallas* in which the character, Bobby Ewing, was absurdly brought back from the dead in a shower in a desperate bid to boost ratings for the show. All the months of Bobby's absence were explained away as a dream!

1   Choose a soap star who has 'died' in a show (e.g. Trisha from *Emmerdale* or Richard Hillman from *Coronation Street*). Imagine the ratings in the show have plummeted since their 'death'. Write a letter to the show's producer on how you can bring this character back to life, and make it convincing to the audience. Make your letter lively, interesting and light hearted. You may wish to begin your letter as follows. (Notice the use of informal, lively vocabulary.)

> Dear Producer,
>
> I was concerned to hear how your show's ratings have gone down since the 'death' of . . . . I believe the only way to boost ratings is if they come back to life. I know it sounds ridiculous yet my suggestions below will not only convince the audience, but help your programme end up back at the top of the ratings – a place where it belongs . . .

2 This radio phone-in is an excellent example of how a debate should be organised. Many opinions are expressed by people with interesting ideas about soaps. To help you plan a piece of discursive writing for Question 3, copy out and continue the table below. One example has been included for each point.

For/ Against	Point made	Evidence	Person giving evidence	Your own views on this point
For	Soaps raise awareness of important issues	I remember after the famous revelation of Mark Fowler having HIV. Aids help-lines said they were inundated with calls.	James	
Against	Children are exposed to the wrong kind of information.	But, certainly, my concern is for those kids that are, sort of, under twelve who are exposed to this at half-past seven at night.	Mike	

3 Using your completed table, produce a piece of discursive writing titled 'Are soaps good for teenagers?' You need to use the arguments from the table as well as your own views on the topic. Remember to use connecting words to help structure your argument. For example:

To add a point	To contradict an argument	To show cause and effect	To summarise or to conclude
in addition, furthermore, moreover, another point is, some people argue	although, but, despite, even though, however, in contrast, in spite of, instead, nevertheless, nonetheless, notwithstanding, on the contrary, on the one hand, on the other hand, regardless, still, though, yet	accordingly, as a result, because, consequently, for this purpose, hence, so, then, therefore, thereupon, thus, to this end	in short, on the whole, therefore, to summarise accordingly, as a result, because, consequently, for this purpose, hence, so, then, therefore, thereupon, thus, to this end

Section B: Teenage Kicks

B1: Kevin the Teenager

Introduction

Harry Enfield is a performer who is very familiar on British television. He is associated with some of the most recognisable comic characters of the last fifteen years. 'Stavros' the kebab shop owner and 'Loadsamoney' brought him to people's attention when they appeared on the Channel Four programmes *Friday Night Live* and *Saturday Night Live* in the 1980s. A succession of series for the BBC in the 1990s have made 'Wayne and Waynetta Slob', 'Tim Nice-But-Dim', 'The Old Gits' and many other characters household names.

'Kevin the Teenager' is typical of the characters that Enfield created with his co-writers of that time, Paul Whitehouse and Charlie Higson. He is grotesque and unpleasant, but might just be based on something quite truthful about people. If this is the case, it explains why characters like 'Kevin and Perry' are as popular as they are.

In this extract, Kevin has not been home all night and his parents are really worried.

Number of parts: 4
Parts in order of appearance:

Father
Mother
Kevin
Perry

Kevin the Teenager

Int. Patterson's living room.

Father is on the phone. Mother is pacing up and down.

FATHER   Ok, Jim. Well if you hear anything – let me know, and I'll do the same. Ok.

Kevin comes through the front door.

MOTHER   Here he is now.

FATHER   Oh, he's just arrived back. I'll call you in a minute.

Pause as Kevin makes to go upstairs. Mother calls after him.

MOTHER   Kevin!

KEVIN   What?

MOTHER   Can you come down here, please?

Pause as he slowly tramps into the living room.

KEVIN   What?

MOTHER   Kevin, where have you been?

KEVIN   Mwhat?

FATHER   It is two o'clock in the afternoon, darling. We've been really worried about you.

KEVIN   Ceeurgh! You are so sick-makingly pathetic!

MOTHER   It's not pathetic. Kevin, we haven't heard a thing from you SINCE YESTERDAY TEATIME! Where did you stay last night?

KEVIN   I went to Perry's, didn't I?

FATHER   Well, you didn't stay at Perry's – I spoke to his mum.

KEVIN   I didn't say I STAYED there – I said I WENT there!

FATHER   Well, Perry's Mum didn't see you all evening.

Slight pause as Kevin's brain starts working overtime.

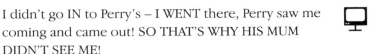

KEVIN I didn't go IN to Perry's – I WENT there, Perry saw me coming and came out! SO THAT'S WHY HIS MUM DIDN'T SEE ME!

Pause as Kevin seethes.

MOTHER So where did you stay?

KEVIN Pete's.

MOTHER Then why did Pete's dad ring us this morning, and ask if Pete was here?

KEVIN Well, I don't know – do I? Why don't you ask HIM?

MOTHER I did. Pete told his parents he was staying here.

Slight pause.

KEVIN So?

MOTHER Well, he didn't, did he? And you didn't stay at Perry's, and you didn't stay at Pete's.

Slight pause before Kevin decides to tough it out.

KEVIN WE DID STAY AT PETE'S!

MOTHER Kevin, I spoke to his dad!

KEVIN WELL, HIS DAD'S A LIAR, THEN!

Slight pause before Kevin decides a small embellishment is due.

KEVIN We stayed at Pete's till eleven.

The doorbell rings.

MOTHER Oh. You stayed there till eleven, did you? And then where did you go?

KEVIN Well, I dunno, do I?

MOTHER Well, I would've thought you were exactly the person to know!

Father answers the door – it's Perry.

FATHER	Hello, Perry – come in.
PERRY	Hello, Mr. Patterson. Good morning, how are you?

Mother spots the chance to catch Kevin out with Perry's sudden appearance.

MOTHER	Ah, Perry!
PERRY	Hello, Mrs. Patterson. Good morning, how are you? (Sort of thing).

Perry goes over to the fridge for a cola.

MOTHER	Afternoon, Perry – had a good night last night?
PERRY	Yes please, Mrs. Patterson. Please. Thank you.
MOTHER	Where'd you stay?
PERRY	My 'ouse.
MOTHER	Oh? Your parents rang, and said you didn't.

Slight pause as Perry catches Kevin mouthing something, silently.

PERRY	Oh, I forgot – Pete's.
MOTHER	You stayed at Pete's.
PERRY	Yes!

Perry is still trying to interpret Kevin's instructions.

PERRY	N-no. Yes or no? Er, I like your dress, Mrs Patterson – is it new?

Perry finally gets it.

PERRY	DAVE'S! We stayed at Dave's!
MOTHER	Oh – you did, did you?
PERRY	Yeah! I forgot Dave wasn't Pete.

Slight pause.

| MOTHER | So you stayed at Dave's – did you Kevin? |
| KEVIN | Y-e-a-h. |

Kevin looks rather smug. The phone rings, and Kevin lunges for it, but Father beats him to it.

| FATHER | Hello? No, Dave's not here. No, I thought he stayed at home last night, with Kevin and Perry. Oh. Ok. Thanks. |

Father replaces receiver, and looks questioningly at Kevin – who's been caught.

KEVIN	Ugh! Ugh! Ugh! ALL RIGHT, WE WENT TO TRACKS!
MOTHER	What, the nightclub? How long did you stay THERE?
KEVIN	*(snorts)* All night, of course. Ceeurgh, what's your problem?
MOTHER	All right, Kevin. All right. I've had enough of this. YOU ARE NOT ALLOWED IN NIGHTCLUBS! You are grounded for two weeks.
KEVIN	W-H-A-T? That's SO UNFAIR!

The phone rings again. Father quickly picks it up.

| FATHER | Hello? Oh, Jane. Yes, we were worried – but he's home now. Well . . . what, he stayed with you? Oh. Well. Thanks for letting me know. |

Father replaces receiver.

FATHER	Oh. Damon's mum said apparently you arrived at her house at eleven thirty, and stayed there all night. Is that true?
PERRY	Kev couldn't get into Tracks. He don't look eighteen.
KEVIN	(Shhhadup!)
PERRY	Me an' the others got in, though.
KEVIN	*(snorts)* (You are dead!)

MOTHER Well it's fine for you to stay at Damon's, Kevin – why didn't you tell us the truth in the first place?

KEVIN Ugh! Ugh! Ugh! Don't be so STUPID! You just DON'T UNDERSTAND DO YOU? HOW COULD I POSSIBLY TELL YOU THE TRUTH? YOU'RE MY PARENTS!

Activities: Kevin the Teenager

1 In this extract we see the conflict between Kevin and his parents. Copy out the table below in which there are examples of Kevin's attitude towards his parents. In pairs, decide and make notes on how these lines should be read out. Then, choose two each and read them out to the class. Remember to reflect his character.

Words used	Facial expression	Position on the set	Tone of voice
Mwhat?			
Ceeurgh! You are so sick-makingly pathetic!			
I didn't say I STAYED there I said I WENT there!			
Well I don't know do I? Why don't you ask HIM?			
WELL, HIS DAD'S A LIAR, THEN! (slight pause before Kevin decides a small embellishment is due)			

Words used	Facial expression	Position on the set	Tone of voice
Ugh! Ugh! Ugh! Don't be so STUPID! You just DON'T UNDERSTAND DO YOU? HOW COULD I POSSIBLY TELL YOU THE TRUTH? YOU'RE MY PARENTS!			

2 Stage directions are an important feature of this extract. These are used to indicate how the lines should be read out and in what way the action should be presented to the audience. It is very helpful in establishing the personality of the characters involved as well as their relationship with others.

Pick out the important dramatic devices and explain what their dramatic effect is. A few have been completed for you below.

Examples	Dramatic effect
(pause as Kevin makes to go upstairs. Mother calls after him) (pause as Kevin slowly tramps into the living room)	Reveals disrespect Kevin has towards parents – he is not even prepared to give them an explanation of his absence.
I didn't say I STAYED there – I said I WENT there	Use of capital letters to emphasise sarcasm and contempt for parents' questioning.

3   In groups of four, write the imaginary conversation in script form
    that the four friends, Kevin, Perry, Pete and Dave, may have had
    before they returned home. The script should reflect their negative
    attitude towards their parents.

    It could start like this:

    KEVIN: *Betta get 'ome – old dears will give me loads of grief.*
    DAVE: *Why? You only stayed at my gaff!*
    PERRY: *Yeh but we don't wanna tell em that, do we?*

4   a) In pairs discuss and present an argument which supports the
        statement:

        Teenagers are unfairly presented in the media.

        Consider:

        • how teenagers are presented
        • what is wrong and unfair about this presentation
        • what problems teenagers face
        • why teenagers should be presented more fairly.

    b) Using these ideas, write an article aimed at adults in which you
        argue this point.

5   Imagine you are Kevin and describe in no more than 150 words
    how he feels about his parents after the script finishes. Use the
    same language as he does in the script. His negative attitude
    needs to come across to the audience.

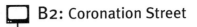

B2: Coronation Street

Introduction

Coronation Street was first broadcast by Granada Television in 1960. It has become one of the most popular soap operas in television history, regularly attracting audiences of over 18 million for its most dramatic storylines.

In recent years, partly because of competition from *EastEnders*, *Home and Away* and *Hollyoaks*, the Street has introduced a number of younger characters. This has led to some controversial issues being written in to the storylines; such as Aidan Critchley being wrongly accused of murder, or Sarah-Louise Platt becoming a teenage mum.

In this episode, broadcast in May 2003, Todd, a very bright lad, has been dumped by his girlfriend, Sarah-Louise, and has decided to leave school without taking his A Levels. He comes home to face his mother after walking out of his first exam. His mum wants him to get top grades in all his exams and to go to Oxford University. She has made a special tea for him and is not expecting him home so early.

Number of parts: 3
Parts in order of appearance:

Mum
Todd
Jason

Coronation Street

Scene: Eileen Grimshaw's house. Front room.

> *Todd, Eileen's son, walks in.*

MUM   Hiya! I didn't expect you so early. How was it? Was it hard?

TODD   Wasn't hard.

MUM   Oh well, it wasn't too easy, was it? I mean, they didn't make it easy on purpose to trick you into thinking it was easy but really it was hard?

TODD   Mam . . .

MUM   Look, sit down and tell me all about it. Do you want a drink?

TODD   No, I'm fine. Mam, I need to tell you something . . . *(Pause)* . . . and you're not going to be 'appy.

MUM   You've made it up with Sarah, haven't you?

TODD   No, it's not about Sarah, it's about me. *(Long pause)* I didn't sit the exam.

MUM   What do you mean? Did you get the date wrong or summat?

TODD   No, it was the right day. I went in to the hall, read the paper but I didn't write anything apart from my name.

MUM   But . . . Why? . . . I don't understand . . .

TODD   Decided not to do it. I'm not doing any of them. I'm not taking my A Levels. I'm not going to Oxford.

MUM   *(smiles)* Yeah, you are! *(She sits down, thinking he is joking.)*

TODD   No, I'm not!

MUM   I don't believe this.

TODD   I know you had big plans for my future and I know I'm a disappointment but . . . it's my life, Mam!

MUM   *(shouts)* YOUR life! YOUR life! Is this some kind of a joke? Because if it is it's not very funny.

TODD   It's not a joke.

MUM   *(shakes her head)* So, you're telling me you've thrown it all away, everything you've worked for, and for what? What have you thrown it away for? Is it her? That little cow across the street, because she's finished with you?

TODD   Don't call her a cow!

MUM   I'll call her what I like!

TODD   It's got nothing to do with Sarah. It's me. It's what I want. And I don't want to go to Oxford.

MUM   Well then, why did you apply there in the first place? Why let us think that's what you wanted when you didn't?

TODD   Because I got carried away with it all, the idea of it. And then there was you . . .

MUM   Oh, so it's my fault . . .

TODD   No, I'm not saying that. I'm saying that you got all excited . . . Oxford . . . Oxford . . . it's all you talk about. I saw it meant a lot to you.

MUM   But it didn't to you. You were just going along with it because you didn't want to upset me?

TODD   Yeh.

MUM   *(shouts)* WELL, I'M UPSET *NOW*! I'm a hundred times more upset than I would have been! Look, this is your future, Todd, You're gonna be a lawyer!

TODD   No, I'm not. I don't wanna be a lawyer!

MUM   What . . . what DO you want to be?

TODD   I don't know.

MUM   Well, maybe I can help you. There's factory work, stacking shelves, dredging the canal. Oh, there's no end of career opportunities for them with no qualifications.

TODD   I've got qualifications.

MUM   Not ones that matter!

Todd's mum gets up and picks up her handbag.

MUM Come on.

TODD Where to?

MUM I'll take you to school. Maybe you can still do your exams.

TODD No, I told you, I'm not doing 'em!

MUM Yes you are, you're doing them if I have to stand over you!

She grabs his arm.

TODD Get off me! I'm not a little kid!

MUM *(screams)* Well, stop behaving like one!

Jason, Todd's brother, comes in to the room.

JASON Let him go!

MUM Have you 'eard what he's done? Has he told you?

No answer.

MUM Well?

JASON Mam, it's his life!

MUM *(imitates Jason)* It's his life! He's just about to ruin his life and that's all you can say?

Todd's mum walks into the kitchen, picks up the trifle she has made for Todd's tea and turns around to face the boys.

MUM Why, oh why do I bother?

She drops the bowl of trifle on to the floor.

Activities: Coronation Street

In this scene the director develops the conflict between Todd and his mum carefully so that the audience is able to identify with the pressures often faced by teenagers. This extract also highlights the feelings of parents whose children do not live up to their expectations. We are shown different aspects of Todd's mum in this scene.

1 Copy out the table below. Then find examples that support the following statements about Mrs Grimshaw's character. A few examples have been completed for you.

Characteristics of Todd's mum	Evidence from script
caring and loving	She has made a special tea for him.
unprepared to accept the truth	
angry and annoyed	Is it her? That little cow across the street, because she's finished with you?
tries to blame others	
sarcastic	
aggressive	
interfering	
won't take responsibility	*Oh, so it's my fault . . .*

2 The writer of this extract is able to create this tension through:
   • dialogue (speech)
   • director's notes
   • actions of characters
   • pauses.

Find examples of these techniques and explain what it reveals about the relationship between Todd and his mum.

Some examples have been done for you below.

Techniques	Evidence	What it reveals about the relationship
Dialogue (speech)	TODD Don't call her a cow! MUM I'll call her what I like!	Todd is finally beginning to stand up for himself and Sarah while his mum is still trying to take control of the situation.
Director's notes		
Actions of characters		
Pauses	TODD No, I'm fine. Mam, I need to tell you something . . . (pause) . . . and you're not going to be 'appy.	The dramatic pause helps the audience to sense the tension and anxiety that Todd is feeling as well as revealing that he is frightened of his mum's reaction.

3   The strain of this conflict has taken its toll on both Todd and his mum. For this task you need to try to empathise with how they must have been feeling before and after this event. Produce a monologue (a written speech delivered by one actor on stage) for *one* of the following scenes:

a) Todd before he enters the house to tell his mum

b) his mum after hearing the news when she is alone in the house.

When delivering your monologue to the class, remember to:

• make eye contact with your audience
• use facial expressions to reflect the character's thoughts and feelings
• use body language to reflect the feelings of anger, relief, tension
• adjust your tone of voice and volume accordingly.

 **B3:** Grange Hill

Introduction

Grange Hill has been a consistent part of the BBC Children's TV schedule for over twenty five years. Many well-known television faces, like Mark Fowler (*Eastenders*), were first seen in the classrooms and corridors of the inner-city comprehensive school at the heart of this enduringly popular tea-time drama.

The programme was created by Phil Redmond, who later produced *Hollyoaks*. Like *Hollyoaks*, *Grange Hill* has tried to reflect real problems which has led to storylines revolving around some sensitive issues.

The following extract is from an episode screened in March 2003.

Number of parts: 5
Parts in order of appearance:

Mr Malachay
Boys
Karen
Maddy
Kathy

Grange Hill

Int. Boys changing room.

> *The changing rooms are in the obligatory state of disarray and Mr Malachay is nowhere to be seen. Abel, Andy and Togger are in the midst of a towel fight with Mooey and a few of his friends. Jeremy is in the corner, diligently hanging his clothes up, desperate not to be caught up in the action.*

MR MALACHAY   What's going on in here?

> *The class stop in their tracks. The class should mouth the words to the following speech – they know it off by heart . . .*

MR MALACHAY   No malarkey, I said. I leave you alone for *two* minutes and I come back to a cage of wild animals.

> *He turns to look at the class. Silence.*

MR MALACHAY   I've a good mind to cancel swimming today . . . (lesson)

> *Chorus of "aw, sir"*

MR MALACHAY   One more chance. And no . . .

BOYS   Malarkey

MR MALACHAY   Right, you've got thirty seconds to get out to the pool.

> *The excited boys scramble to get out to the pool. One of the boys throws a towel over Jeremy's head. Mr Malachay removes the towel from his head.*

MR MALACHAY   Silly boy.

Cut to Ext. Playground bench.

> *Maddie and Karen are sat on the bench outside the school entrance.*

KAREN   So you got anyone else lined up?

MADDIE   *(false bravado)* Plenty of options, just don't want to rush into anything.

KAREN   So d'you really think Baz is seeing someone else?

MADDIE   He wouldn't dare. *(Beat)* if he was, I'd kill her. And then I'd kill him.

KAREN   So you're over him, then.

MADDIE   Definitely . . .

> *Beat.*

MADDIE   . . . he was pretty fit though.

KAREN   *(plays it down)* I guess.

MADDIE   Better than the rest of the spods in our year.

KAREN   Maybe.

MADDIE   And he did used to make me laugh . . . *(drifting off)* and he used to look so cute when he was angry. There was this one time . . .

KAREN   Maddie . . .

MADDIE   But he's history. That's it. No more Baz.

> *Maddie and Karen are lost in their own thoughts. That is until Karen notices Kathy sat on the other side of the school yard, looking sad.*

KAREN   Don't look like you're the only one depressed. Check it out. *(Motions to Kathy)* Do you reckon we should have some fun?

MADDIE   I think we had enough fun the last week. I kind of feel sorry for her *(registers the shock from Karen)* . . . must be my hormones or something.

Maddie and Karen head over to Kathy

MADDIE   *(to Kathy)* You alright?

Kathy just shrugs. The two girls sit either side of her.

MADDIE   This wouldn't be about the freak of nature again would it?

Again Kathy just shrugs

MADDIE   *(despair)* Look we've been through this. You told him how you felt and he messed up. *(Matter of fact)* you just got to forget about him and find someone else.

KATHY   *(simply)* But I don't want anyone else.

MADDIE   What's gone wrong now?

KATHY   He just doesn't want to speak to me. I wish I'd never said anything, one minute he was my best friend and now . . . it's like . . . *(she tails off)*

MADDIE   So you still like him then?

Kathy nods.

MADDIE   Then how about you leave it to me. *(Beat – justifying herself)* It's obvious you two are incapable of getting yourselves together . . .

KATHY   *(worried)* What are you going to say to him?

MADDIE   I don't know, yet. I can't sit down and talk to the boy, can I? He's a freak. I don't even know why you want to go out with him

KATHY   *(simply)* Because I like him.

MADDIE   Yeah, alright leave it to me. Just because my love life's a disaster, doesn't mean yours has to be.

KATHY   What about Baz?

MADDIE   *(hard)* Baz who?

On Maddie – a girl on a mission. Determined to sort out the mess that is Kathy and Martin.

Synopses of the following scenes

Int. Living room. Day.

Baz tries to reassure his sister, Annie, that they can manage their sick father. She talks about missing her mother.

Int. Swimming pool. Day.

Jeremy gets knocked in the pool because of Mooey. Mr Malachey saves Jeremy and blames Togger for the incident.

Ext. School. Day.

Female sixth-former talks to boy she fancies about joining the drama club that he is already in.

Int. Changing rooms. Day.

Jeremy tells Togger that he's as bad as Mooey in terms of picking on him. Togger suggests that Jeremy try harder to fit in with his new school friends.

Int. Changing rooms. Day.

Amy asks Anika to test her on her History A level revision. Amy can't remember anything that she revised all weekend.

Int. Swimming pool. Day.

> *Tanya and friend float something unseen into the pool.*

Ext. School yard. Day

> *Maddy tells Ron that they should combine to get Kathy and Martin together.*

Int. Corridor. Day.

> *Tanya claims the prize underpants from Togger for completing a dare. Togger and Andy tell Tanya she can't have them as she broke the rules by laughing at the pants.*

Ext. Street. Day.

> *Anika apologises to Amy for upsetting her with the revision test. Amy is inconsolable and still upset about losing her Mum at such a difficult time in her life.*

Int. Swimming pool. Day.

> *Mr Malachay comes into the pool to pin a notice on the board. He sees a canoe floating in the pool with a model skeleton inside it. Attached to its chest is a sign which reads 'No Malarkey'.*

Activities: Grange Hill

1 In these opening scenes the audience are given a slice of school life from the perspectives of teenagers. The first scene involves the PE teacher, Mr Malachey, confronting a group of boys who are messing about in the boys changing rooms.

a) In groups of four, take the roles of Mr Malachey and three of the boys who are in the changing rooms and discuss the following:

- What costumes would each of the characters wear to reflect their personalities?
- What should the body language of the characters be? Aggressive? Frightened?
- How should the characters read out their lines? Consider tone of voice, volume and intonation. Which words should be emphasised and why?

You may include extra dialogue to help create the atmosphere.

b) Now act out the scene, making sure that you take on the advice that has been given to you by your group.

2 The boys in this scene are mischievous, whereas the girls are more interested in their love life! Maddy's character is shown to be defensive; she is upset about 'Baz' but is trying not to show it.

a) In pairs, discuss the reasons why teenagers often hide their emotions from their friends.

b) With your partner, reveal what you believe Maddy is really thinking during this scene. This is called 'thought tracking'. You need to explain what you believe Maddy is feeling inside. Now take on the role of the two 'Maddys'. The Maddy that her mates see and hear should be sitting down reading out her lines, while 'the real Maddy' walks around her describing her real thoughts. For example:

> Maddy's lines: 'Plenty of options. I just don't want to rush into anything yet.'

Maddy's thoughts: 'I can't believe he's left me. I'm never gonna find someone else.'

3 a) In this extract we see the type of problems that teenagers face in school. Decide on five issues that you feel are difficult to deal with in school, e.g. bullying, making new friends, coping with homework.

   b) Using these ideas produce an advice leaflet for Year 6 pupils coming to your school, in which you must provide helpful advice on how to cope with the challenges of life at secondary school.

   Remember to include the following in your advice leaflet:

   - headlines
   - sub-headings
   - facts and opinions
   - helpful advice
   - pictures/captions.

Section C: Scary Movies

C1: House of Dracula

Introduction

The original story of *Dracula* was written by Bram Stoker and published in 1897. Since then the infamous vampire has appeared in over one hundred films, always appearing only at night and kept alive by the blood of innocent people. Universal Studios have made some of the most famous horror films to feature monsters, many of which, like Dracula and Frankenstein, were made in the 1930s. *House of Dracula* was made by Universal in 1945 as a follow up to *House of Frankenstein*.

The following extract is from early in the film. It opens as Dracula pays a late-night visit to a scientist called Dr Edelmann, famous for his near-miraculous cures of hopeless cases. The Count persuades the scientist to help him seek a release from the horrific curse that makes him want to kill. The question is whether Dracula genuinely desires a cure or if he has another goal in mind.

Number of parts: 4
Parts in order of appearance:

Meliza Morelle (*doesn't speak*)
Dracula
Doctor Franz Edelmann
Bartholemew (*doesn't speak*)

House of Dracula

Fade in.

Int. Miliza's bedroom. Night. **Med. shot.**

> *The ANGLE is toward a pair of open French windows through which a giant bat is seen flying across Edelmann's garden toward CAMERA. As it comes into a **CLOSE SHOT** and hovers toward the window, chittering softly while it looks **o.s.** with glittering eyes, the CAMERA PANS AWAY to another part of the room where shadows of the creature's wings beat upon the wall beyond the bed in which lies a girl, Meliza Morelle. Her face, revealed in the moonlight streaming in through the window, is beautiful. Reacting subconsciously to the o.s. SOUNDS of the bat's chittering, MELIZA stirs restively.*

Med. shot. At window.

> *The bat's wings beat the air silently for a few seconds longer, while in a **DISSOLVE** its form melts away into a rapidly attenuating fog which transmutes itself into a man who, by virtue of his traditional attire, is recognisable as DRACULA. He admires Meliza a moment, then moves away.*

Ext. Edelmann's garden. **Full shot.**

> *DRACULA walks down steps and across the garden toward the French windows of a room on the lower floor.*

Int. Edelmann's study. Med. shot.

> *ANGLING into the garden through a French window (closed). DRACULA enters, peers through window as CAMERA ANGLES to DOCTOR FRANZ EDELMANN, a man whose face*

reflects the gentle compassion of one who has devoted his life to helping suffering humanity, seated in a chair beside his desk, dozing. There is an open book upon the arm of the chair. A large cat, BARTHOLEMEW, is curled upon his lap, asleep.

Close shot. Dracula.

At the window, his eyes fixed upon Edelmann, o.s. He glances towards the book Edelmann has been reading.

Insert. Book.

Its title reads: ADVENTURES IN THE SUPERNATURAL.

Closeup. Dracula.

The CAMERA ANGLES with him as he comes through the doorway into —

Int. Edelmann's study. Med. Full shot.

This WIDER ANGLE reveals that the room is furnished comfortably in the manner of a doctor's office. DRACULA, entering from the garden terrace, comes down-scene and pauses when a little distance from the desk. As he contemplates the sleeping man, the cat awakens suddenly . . .

Close shot. Bartholemew.

As the animal looks o.s., its hair bristles. Spitting fear, he arches his back, then jumps off Edelmann's lap and runs out into the garden . . .

Med. Close shot. Edelmann and Dracula.

The sudden movement of the cat jumping from his lap causes EDELMANN to stir. EDELMANN opens his eyes – staring at the intruder.

EDELMANN What are you doing here! Who are you!?

DRACULA I am Baron Latos – I have come to you for help –

EDELMANN *(he glances off-stage at clock)* – But – it's five o'clock in the morning!

DRACULA I must apologise for the intrusion. But travel for me is extremely difficult and I have come a long way.

EDELMANN I do not understand!

DRACULA Perhaps you will after you have lead me to the basement room of this castle!

EDELMANN What do you mean?

DRACULA Have no fear, Doctor. Had conditions permitted, I would have presented myself in the usual manner.

EDELMANN It *is* most unusual!

DRACULA I will explain everything to you before sunrise.

EDELMANN, obviously mystified, follows DRACULA toward the door –

The Great Hall. Med. **Moving shot.**

EDELMANN lights the candles in the candelabrum and proceeds across the hall toward door followed by DRACULA.

DRACULA Doctor Edelmann, do you believe in the immortality of the soul?

EDELMANN I'm a religious man.

DRACULA Of the body . . . ?

EDELMANN	*(a slight shrug)* Medical science refutes such a thing.
DRACULA	Just as it denies the existence of vampirism?
EDELMANN	It doesn't deny certain physical aspects of it. Cases have been recorded in which the victims – driven by some abnormal urge – actually believed that blood was necessary to keep them alive and became psychopathic killers to get it. *(Professionally)* These beliefs probably upset their metabolism – brought about chemical changes which induced false beliefs and lustful appetites. *(With a gesture)* The whole thing is of a highly speculative nature – particularly the supernatural aspects.
DRACULA	You doubt the supernatural . . . ?
EDELMANN	– I find it difficult to believe that a human being can change himself into a bat, or that by feeding on the blood of the living he can attain eternal life.

They have stopped at the door to the basement stairway which EDELMANN is unlocking. Suddenly he turns to DRACULA suspiciously.

| EDELMANN | But what has this discussion to do with us, Baron Latos –? |
| DRACULA | *(cryptically)* A great deal, perhaps. Shall we proceed, Doctor? |

Somewhat reluctantly, EDELMANN opens the door and they EXIT.

Int. Basement room. Night. Full shot.

*EDELMANN enters carrying a **candelabrum**. As DRACULA and EDELMANN descend the stairs, into the room, the CAMERA **TRACKS IN**, stopping in a MED. CLOSE SHOT when*

*EDELMANN and DRACULA reach a point where a coffin of
ancient pattern rests upon a couple of broken blocks of
masonry. EDELMANN reacts.*

Close shot. Edelmann and Dracula.

EDELMANN, startled, is staring at the coffin.

EDELMANN　The Dracula Crest!

*DRACULA, smiling slightly, extends his right hand and
points to the ring he wears.*

Close shot. Dracula's hands.

*The large ring on his second finger carries a crested Coat of
Arms, that of the House of Dracula.*

Closeup. Dracula.

DRACULA　*(quietly)* Yes, Doctor . . . you see before you a man
who has lived for centuries – kept alive by the blood
of innocent people.

Med. Close two shot.

EDELMANN　*(with a sceptical smile)* You ask me to believe that?

DRACULA　*(pleadingly)* That is why I've come here – to seek
release from a curse of misery and horror against
which I am powerless to fight alone.

Close shot. Edelmann.

Intrigued, EDELMANN takes a few steps toward the coffin.

EDELMANN   According to legend, a vampire must return to his grave before sun up. If you were to remain here, how would that be possible?

Two shot. Edelmann and Dracula.

DRACULA   Within this coffin is a layer of soil taken from my birthplace . . . That earth makes this my grave – in which I must lie helpless during the daylight hours.

EDELMANN   *(tolerantly)* Because one ray of sunlight falling upon a vampire would destroy him – ?

DRACULA   Yes, Doctor . . .

EDELMANN looks toward the direction of their entrance, and then at DRACULA with a return of his annoyance and resentment.

EDELMANN   The door of this room was locked . . . *(Indicating the coffin)* How did you get in here?

DRACULA   *(smiling slightly)* Since you do not believe in the supernatural, let us say that you were mistaken, that the outer door was not locked.

EDELMANN   You've taken a great deal for granted, Baron . . . Proceeding on the assumption that I would take your case.

DRACULA   Your reputation for helping others made me certain you would . . .

*A glint of **shrewd** calculation comes into DRACULA's eyes as he draws closer to Edelmann.*

Closer shot. The two.

DRACULA   Whatever the cause of my condition, could you effect a cure?

EDELMANN   There might be a way – despite the dangers involved – It would be a *challenge* to medical science –

DRACULA   Accept the challenge, Doctor! Release me from this curse of misery and horror – against which I am powerless to fight alone!

EDELMANN stands pondering the subject without answering as DRACULA glances toward the casement window. Half turning, he gestures toward it.

DRACULA   You must decide quickly, Doctor – before the dawn.

*While EDELMANN is still debating the subject, the CAMERA LEAVES them, **PANNING UP** to the casement window showing a shaft of light which foretells the approach of dawn as we **DISSOLVE OUT**.*

Activities: House of Dracula

1   In this extract, the atmosphere and mood is created without a
    detailed description of the setting or characters. The mood of
    apprehension and tension is developed through the varied
    use of:

    - camera angles
    - sound effects
    - movement of the characters.

    Find another example of each technique and record them in the
    table below. One example has already been completed for each
    technique.

How mood is created without dialogue	Examples
Camera angles	*The ANGLE is toward a pair of open French windows through which a giant bat is seen flying across Edelmann's garden toward CAMERA.*
Sound effects	*Reacting subconsciously to the o.s. SOUNDS of the bat's chittering, Meliza stirs restively.*
Movement of the characters	*Dracula admires Meliza a moment, then moves away.*

2   The director's notes (stage directions) are vital for establishing the
    mood of the scene. With a partner, rewrite the stage directions
    below to create a more sinister mood. On the next page two stage
    directions have been rewritten as examples.

    Be ready to explain your choices to the rest of the class.

Original script	Stage directions changed to create a more sinister and dark mood
CLOSE SHOT – EDELMANN AND DRACULA	CLOSE SHOT – EDELMANN AND DRACULA
Edelmann, startled, is staring at the coffin.	Edelmann, **terrified beyond belief**, is staring at the coffin.
EDELMANN The Dracula Crest!	EDELMANN The Dracula Crest!
Dracula, smiling slightly, extends his right hand and points to the ring he wears.	Dracula extends his right hand, **callously smiling** and points to the ring he wears.
CLOSE SHOT – DRACULA'S HANDS	
The large ring on his second finger carries a crested Coat of Arms, that of the House of Dracula.	
CLOSEUP – DRACULA	
DRACULA (quietly) Yes, Doctor . . . you see before you a man who has lived for centuries — kept alive by the blood of innocent people.	
MED. CLOSE TWO SHOT	
EDELMANN (with a sceptical smile) You ask me to believe that?	
DRACULA (pleadingly) That is why I've come here – to seek release from a curse of misery and horror against which I am powerless to fight alone.	

3   Within a film script, the director's notes must be very concise (straight to the point) and clear for the actors. For example Dr Edelmann is described as:

> *a man whose face reflects the gentle compassion of one who has devoted his life to helping suffering humanity, seated in a chair beside his desk, dozing.*

From your knowledge of Dracula from this scene, produce four lines of description which you believe best reflects his appearance and personality.

4   In this extract, the director wants the audience to sympathise with Dracula's situation, even though they know he kills innocent people regularly! Find evidence of this bid for sympathy and explain how it encourages the audience to view Dracula in a more positive light. An example has been done for you.

Evidence	How this creates sympathy for Dracula
I must apologise for the intrusion. But travel for me is extremely difficult and I have come a long way.	This reveals Dracula as being sensitive and polite.

5   Using the different terms for camera shots and angles in the script, select two minutes of footage from a film you know well and have access to on video or DVD. Then write the stage directions that you think should go with the extract.

C2: Wallace and Gromit

Introduction

The **stop-frame animation** films of Nick Park and Aardman are very popular with both children and adults. Each film has two central characters: Wallace, an inventor, and Gromit, his faithful but put-upon dog. Although he is a dog, Gromit is given human characteristics. For example, he can read the newspaper and one of his hobbies is knitting. This is called 'personification' (where an animal or thing is given human characteristics) and is a literary device often used by comedy writers.

Gromit often gets Wallace out of trouble in their adventures. *A Close Shave* features a robot dog called Preston who gets out of the control of his owner, Wendolene. He starts to make dog-food out of stolen sheep. His character is influenced by the robot in the film *Terminator.*

This extract comes as Wallace and Gromit receive an unwanted visitor and the offer of window-cleaning work. (Because of the way this stop-frame animation is filmed, the script is split into a number of very short **sequences**, labelled 1A, B, C, etc.)

Number of parts: 5
Parts in order of appearance:

Wallace
Gromit (*doesn't speak*)
Lamb (*doesn't speak*)
Preston *(doesn't speak)*
Wendolene

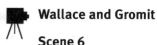 **Wallace and Gromit**

Scene 6

[Sequence]

1. Int. Wallace's bedroom. Night

> ***FADE IN*** *ON WALLACE in bed snoring. We hear the*
> *approach of a heavy lorry. Pan across to Wallace's late*
> *night snack on the bedside table – a plate of cheese and*
> *crackers. The rumble of the truck causes the cheese*
> *knife to fall off the plate – it lands upright in one of the*
> *floorboards, narrowly missing Wallace's slippers.*

1a. Gromit's bedroom. Night.

> *ANGLE ON GROMIT in bed awake with a cup of cocoa*
> *and his knitting. We see the beam of the lorry headlights*
> *arc across his room . . . His ball of wool falls off the*
> *bedside table and ripples appear in his cocoa.*

2. Ext. Town street. Night.

> *ANGLE ON The lorry approaching the traffic lights.*
> *The hiss of brakes.*

2a. Int. Gromit's bedroom. Night.

> *GROMIT's reaction to the sounds.*

2b. Ext. Town street. Night.

> *ANGLE ON The lorry stopping at the traffic lights.*

ANOTHER ANGLE On the side of the truck where a LAMB in the trailer with other sheep is trying to squeeze its way out between the slats of the sheep transporter . . .

He manages to get out and drops down onto the road.

ANOTHER ANGLE The LAMB makes for cover.

ANGLE ON THE WING MIRROR We see PRESTON, the driver, seeing the LAMB escape.

3. Ext. Rear of 62 Wallaby Street. Night.

The LAMB running TOWARDS CAMERA.

The LAMB approaches a garden door.

The frightened LAMB dives into it for cover and up to the backdoor and then pushes his way through Gromit's dog flap.

We see on the garden door the number '62' and above that a sign saying WALLACE 'N' GROMIT'S WASH 'N' GO WINDOW CLEANING SERVICE

RESUME The DRIVER of the truck. He starts to get out of the truck. A hand stops him – a WOMAN's hand . . .

THEN . . .

*His **POV** of the telephone number on the sign in the wing mirror.*

ANOTHER ANGLE The mysterious DRIVER writes the number on his pad – we see he is wearing a distinctive black leather studded wrist band.

RESUME GROMIT who waits for the engine noise to fade into the distance before continuing with his knitting . . . then he runs out of wool . . .

4. Ext. Rear of Wallace & Gromit's house. Day.

Establishing shot of the house.

> *We see the window cleaning sign.*

5. Int. Wallace & Gromit's house. Dining room. Day.

> *GROMIT reading a newspaper, the headlines 'WOOL RATIONING' followed by – 'MORE SHEEP RUSTLING'.*
>
> *The buzzing from Wallace's bedroom, 'BREAKFAST'.*

5a. Int. Wallace's bedroom. Day.

WALLACE   Porridge today eh? Tuesday –

5b. Int. Dining room. Day.

> *GROMIT puts his newspaper down and pulls the breakfast lever. He then looks over at the table awaiting Wallace's arrival. WALLACE is tipped down through the opening in the ceiling and onto his chair.*

WALLACE   Geronimo!

> *ANGLE ON The porridge gun – like something from the **Maginot Line** – steaming and waiting to **eject** its porridge.*
>
> *ANGLE ON WALLACE being dressed. A bowl is on the table in front of him.*
>
> *There is a PFUMPF!*
>
> *The porridge cannon shoots a ball – it lands squarely on the bowl before WALLACE, who smiles at its accuracy – then without warning another PFUMPF!*

CLOSE ON GROMIT looking worried.

WALLACE quickly gets another bowl and catches the next porridge blob – then another PFUMPF! Then another!

WALLACE keeps on catching the porridge blobs until he runs out of bowls –

WALLACE   Ye oow! oh!

ANOTHER ANGLE ON GROMIT, he is already at the back of the porridge cannon.

CLOSE ON The wires at the back – all chewed up.

*WALLACE meanwhile is like a **demented** goalkeeper trying to limit the damage.*

WALLACE   Turn it off!

One splats in his face. He licks it off –

GROMIT manages to turn the machine off and stands there holding the severed wires.

WALLACE   . . . Er – Mice d'you think?

GROMIT suddenly turns and looks at the open door – nothing there. He looks up at WALLACE who moves off towards the pantry.

WALLACE   I think I'll make my own porridge.

GROMIT moves out into the hall and passes a rubber plant with a bite out of one of the leaves.

6. Int. Pantry. Day.

WALLACE moves into the pantry.

He picks up the box of porridge oats and finds that a chunk has been bitten out – teeth marks.

A trail of porridge falling out of the hole.

WALLACE   Well I'll be –

WALLACE lifts the lid off the cheese dish – more marks on the piece of cheese underneath!

He turns towards Gromit with suspicion.

WALLACE   Have y'been peckish during the night? Only someone's been at me cheese!

GROMIT turns away with disdain.

7. Int. Hall. Day.

We see the LAMB pass by in the background just before GROMIT moves off down the hall again and discovers that the plant has now been bitten off at the root – GROMIT is aghast!

GROMIT turns again . . . nothing there . . . except a single leaf just settling in the doorway.

GROMIT moves off into the kitchen.

8. Int. Dining room. Day.

WALLACE, to avoid any confrontation, opens up the newspaper to read it –

He is looking through a bite hole!

He puts his feet up on what he thinks is a **pouffe** *. . .*

WALLACE fails to see that it is in fact the LAMB . . . chewing the stuffing from the real pouffe . . .

WALLACE raises his newspaper – we see the remnants of the headline –

'MORE SHEEP RUSTLING'!

He looks through the hole at GROMIT, who is as nonplussed as he is.

WALLACE Think we should get the – ah Pest Control people in?

The telephone rings . . .

WALLACE, his feet still up on the sheep picks up the receiver.

He presses the loudspeaker button.

GROMIT comes to the door.

Then we hear – WALLACE's best voice.

WALLACE Hello? Wallace and Gromit's wash 'n' go window cleaning service! May we be of assistance?

9. Int. Hallway. Day.

GROMIT listening to the voice on the loudspeaker – a WOMAN's voice faltering and nervous.

WENDOLENE'S Hello? Yes, my windows could do with a jolly good
VOICE OOV clean. The Wool Shop in the High Street – soon as you can.

WALLACE gives GROMIT a thumbs up sign and GROMIT goes to the lever which operates the breakfast sequence and pulls it down to 'Window cleaning' which flashes on and off causing the whole place to flash on/off red!

ON SOUND The whooping emergency claxon !!!!!!!!!

WALLACE On our way madam!

But WALLACE is already rising . . .

10. Int. Dining room. Day.

*To suitably **strident** music Wallace's chair slides back towards the wall leaving the LAMB awestruck by the proceedings.*

Wallace's chair rises majestically up to the ceiling where a flap opens – WALLACE is tipped into the opening.

11. Int. Hollow behind walls. Day.

A hollow behind the walls of number 62.

WALLACE slithers down a slider – head first – and connects with a waiting crash helmet – the slide tips the other way and he slips towards waiting overalls, bucket, sponges and mops . . .

He drops into a pair of Wellington boots.

Then on down into –

12. Int. Window cleaning launch area. Day.

WALLACE arrives at the launch area and is arrested by a bungee then deposited on the seat of a motorcycle combination.

Activities: Wallace and Gromit

1 A screenplay is the actual script of the film. As you can see, it is
written in quite a complex way with lots of action happening at the
same time. To understand how the action develops, choose 10–15
lines of the script and organise the events under the following
headings. One example has been done for you.

Sequence	Time	Place	Action	Camera angle	Sound effects	Dialogue
5B	DAY	DINING ROOM	*GROMIT . . . pulls breakfast lever . . . WALLACE is tipped down through the opening in the ceiling and onto his chair.*	*ANGLE ON porridge gun*	*PUMPF*	*WALLACE Geronimo!*

2 The relationship between Wallace and Gromit is the strength of the
script. The banter and humour they have is the reason for much of
Nick Park's success.

   a) Find three more examples of Wallace's silly behaviour that are
   matched with Gromit's concern.

Wallace's silly behaviour	Gromit's concern
'Er – Mice d'you think?	*GROMIT suddenly turns and looks at the open door – nothing there.*

b) Using the information in 2a and your own thoughts on the two characters, write the conversation they might have about their latest job as window cleaners.

3 The appeal of this extract comes through the actions of the characters, the dialogue, the rapid sequence shifts and the humour.

   a) Choose your *three* favourite pieces of:
   - action
   - dialogue
   - quick scene change
   - humour.

   b) Explain why you think these appeal to the audience.

4 Choose one section from the script and rewrite it as a piece of fiction. Use the example below as a guide for how to change a film script to a piece of literary fiction.

   > The bedroom quivers with Wallace's snoring. The sound of the heavy lorry in the distance is invading the room. Last night's supper of cheese and crackers is disturbed through the rumble of the truck outside. The cheese knife falls dramatically, just missing Wallace's slippers.

5 In pairs, write what you think would happen in Sequence 13 where Wallace begins the window cleaning job at Wendolene's shop. Remember to use the following techniques in your script:
   - stage directions
   - camera angles
   - dialogue
   - rapid sequence changes
   - humour
   - disasters.

C3: North by Northwest

Introduction

North By Northwest was written by Ernest Lehman and directed by
Alfred Hitchcock in 1959. Hitchcock, an English director, was known as
the master of suspense and *North by Northwest* was one of his most
popular romantic thrillers.

The following extract is from near the end of the film. The villain,
Phillip Vandamm, is a foreign spy who believes that the hero, Roger
Thornhill, is a CIA agent named Kaplan. Eve, Vandamm's girlfriend, is
the real CIA agent. She has just shot Thornhill/Kaplan in a crowded
café with a blank bullet. The shooting was a stunt to prove Eve's
loyalty to Vandamm. Thornhill, who has fallen in love with Eve, has
followed her to Vandamm's house as he fears that she will be
discovered.

The scene opens with Vandamm discussing his next move with his
accomplice, Leonard.

Number of parts: 4
Parts in order of appearance:

Vandamm
Leonard
Eve
Thornhill *(doesn't speak)*

North by Northwest

Outside the window.

> *THORNHILL watches as EVE goes up to the balcony.
> LEONARD stares at her all the way, and VANDAMM peers at
> him, sensing hostility in his attitude. When EVE disappears
> into one of the bedrooms, VANDAMM addresses LEONARD
> with a trace of facetiousness.*

VANDAMM   Well, Leonard – how does one say farewell to one's
own right arm?

LEONARD   In your case, sir, I'm afraid you're going to wish you
had cut it off sooner . . .

> *During the above interchange, THORNHILL will glance
> sharply up to his right when he sees the lights go on in the
> balcony bedroom window, and then EVE herself appear for a
> moment at the window. The voices in the living room
> dwindle to an unintelligible drone as THORNHILL backs
> away from the open living room window towards the end of
> the cantilever beam. He is now in a better position to attract
> Eve's attention. He glances about for a pebble to throw, but
> he is too far above ground to reach one. He takes a coin from
> his pocket, glances cautiously towards the living room, then
> looks up and throws the coin at Eve's window. It hits noisily
> and falls to the ground below.*

Intercut several angles.

> *EVE appears at the window, looks out for a moment, then
> walks away.*

> *THORNHILL takes another coin from his pocket, throws it at
> the window and hits again.*

> *EVE appears at the window, opens it and looks out.*

Just as THORNHILL starts to call to her, he glances sharply towards the living room.

LEONARD is walking briskly over to the open living room window. In a moment he will see THORNHILL.

THORNHILL ducks back into the shadows against the house.

LEONARD peers out of the living room window to see the cause of the noise he had heard; EVE continues to look out of the bedroom window. THORNHILL cannot move out to signal her. Seeing nothing, EVE closes the window again and walks away.

THORNHILL glances towards the living room window and his eyes widen:

LEONARD has moved away from the window and, with his back to Vandamm, is taking a gun from his pocket and placing it on a table near the window, as VANDAMM talks in the background, his words unintelligible.

THORNHILL edges up to the window, as LEONARD turns around, the gun concealed on the table behind him. The dialogue becomes intelligible again.

Intercut int. living-room & close ups of Thornhill listening.

LEONARD   You must have had *some* doubts about her yourself, and *still do* –

VANDAMM   *(disturbed and trying to conceal it)* Rubbish . . .

LEONARD   – Why else would you have decided not to tell her that our little treasure here . . . *(Patting the figure of the Tarascan warrior.)* . . . has a bellyful of microfilm?

VANDAMM   *(angrily)* *You* seem to be trying to fill *mine* with rotten apples.

LEONARD   Sometimes the truth does taste like a mouthful of worms, sir.

VANDAMM	*(snorts)* What truth? I've heard nothing but **innuendoes**.
LEONARD	Call it my woman's intuition if you will, but I've never trusted neatness. Neatness is always the result of deliberate planning.
VANDAMM	*(defensively)* She shot him in a moment of fear and anger. You were there. You saw it.
LEONARD	*(nods)* And thereby wrapped everything up into one very neat and tidy bundle:

During the preceding speech, he picks up the gun, holds it behind his back and advances further into the room, the camera following through the window.

LEONARD	A. She removed any doubts you might have had about – what did you call it? – her *'devotion'* and B. She gave herself a new and *urgent* reason to be taken over to the other side with you, just in *case* you decided to change your mind.

VANDAMM manages a laugh, but it is not very convincing.

VANDAMM	You know what *I* think? I think you're jealous of her. I mean it. And I'm touched, dear boy. Really touched.

Suddenly LEONARD brings the gun out from behind his back and points it at the startled VANDAMM.

VANDAMM	*(sharply)* Leonard!

*LEONARD pulls the trigger, fires **point-blank** at VANDAMM. There is a sharp report. VANDAMM stands there, stunned but unharmed.*

LEONARD	*(softly)* The gun she shot Kaplan with. I found it in her luggage.

Waist shot: Vandamm.

> *The camera is very high, looking down on him. As the full realisation of what this means sinks in, the camera slowly descends to examine his expression, and the angle becomes a big head. VANDAMM's reaction is carefully controlled. He is too big a man to let LEONARD see the humiliation and anger he feels at having been duped by Eve.*

LEONARD'S VOICE *(during above)* It's an old Gestapo trick. Shoot one of your own people to show that you're not one of them. They've just freshened it up a bit with blank cartridges.

> *VANDAMM gives a little sigh.*

VANDAMM What a pity . . .

> *From upstairs, the sound of a door opening. VANDAMM looks up, and his brooding expression quickly changes to a wistful smile.*

VANDAMM Ready, dear?

Close shot: Eve.

> *Standing at the balcony railing looking down at him.*

EVE I thought I heard a shot . . .

Full shot: The living-room.

VANDAMM *(calmly)* Yes . . . so did we . . . *(Moves towards the window.)* Must have been a car backfiring or something. *(Looks out)* Hurry down, pet. Almost time to go.

EVE In a moment.

She goes back into her room. LEONARD moves at VANDAMM, speaking in a harsh voice.

LEONARD   You're not taking her on that plane with you?

VANDAMM   Of course I am.

LEONARD stares at him. VANDAMM looks back at him the way an adult looks at a small boy.

VANDAMM   Like our friends, I too believe in neatness, Leonard. *(A pause)* This matter is best disposed of from a great height . . . over water.

Activities: North by Northwest

1 In this extract the director, Alfred Hitchcock, cleverly creates tension through his use of camera angles, editing and dialogue. The table below gives examples of these techniques.

Copy and complete column three by explaining how each technique helps to create the tense mood.

Techniques used	Examples	How this creates tension
Camera angle	*THORNHILL will glance sharply up to his right when he sees the lights go on in the balcony bedroom window . . .*	The camera angle is from Thornhill's point of view. This helps the audience to feel his emotions and the unease that he must be feeling.
Editing	*Just as THORNHILL starts to call to her, he glances sharply towards the living room. LEONARD is walking briskly over to the open living room window. In a moment he will see THORNHILL. THORNHILL ducks back into the shadows against the house.*	
Dialogue	VANDAMM Well, Leonard – how does one say farewell to one's own right arm? LEONARD In your case, sir, I'm afraid you're going to wish you had cut it off sooner . . .	

2 Much of the action takes place between Vandamm and Leonard who are discussing Eve's shooting of Kaplan. The camera angles and director's notes help the audience to imagine what the characters must be feeling. Change the extract in the table below into a piece of descriptive writing.

Include descriptions of the following:

- character's appearance
- character's feelings
- place.

Script version	Descriptive writing
Suddenly LEONARD brings the gun out from behind his back and points it at the startled VANDAMM.	
VANDAMM (*sharply*) Leonard!	
LEONARD pulls the trigger, fires point-blank at VANDAMM. There is a sharp report. VANDAMM stands there, stunned but unharmed.	
LEONARD (*softly*) The gun she shot Kaplan with. I found it in her luggage.	
WAIST SHOT: VANDAMM	
The camera is very high, looking down on him. As the full realization of what this means sinks in, the camera slowly descends to examine his expression, and the angle becomes a big head. VANDAMM's reaction is carefully controlled. He is too big a man to let LEONARD see the humiliation and anger he feels at having been duped by Eve.	

3 In groups of five you need to act out this scene as a piece of drama.

   a) Decide who will take the following parts:

       • Director
       • Thornhill
       • Vandamm
       • Leonard
       • Eve.

   b) Prepare for your performance by:

       • re-reading the script, taking your chosen roles
       • producing a storyboard of the script, which includes stage directions and character's positions on stage
       • discussing in rehearsal how the scene should be staged and how lines should be said (the director's role)
       • learning your lines and performing.

       Watch as groups perform the scene and be ready to offer comments on how a performance might be improved.

Section D: Live and Spontaneous

D1: Live Football Commentary

Introduction

One of the hardest jobs in broadcasting is the live radio commentary.
On television, commentators can sometimes let the pictures do the
talking. On radio, the commentator has to describe everything: the
ground, the crowd, the action, the players, the referee, the linesman,
the atmosphere. Pausing for a few seconds is not an option. It is a job
that many people think they would be able to do but in fact requires
great skill and co-ordination.

It is made even harder when commentators have to speak over a huge
and very noisy crowd, as they do in the following extract. It is taken
from Radio Five Live commentary of the match at Ibrox Park in
Scotland, when Glasgow Rangers met Manchester United in the so-
called 'Battle of Britain' on Wednesday, 22 October 2003.

The commentator is Alan Green and the summarisers are Peter
Schmeichel and Terry Butcher.

Number of parts: 3
Parts in order of appearance:

Alan Green
Peter Schmeichel
Terry Butcher

Live Football Commentary

Manchester United lead with a minute to go. Rangers throw everything forward in an attempt to get an equaliser.

GREEN   . . . good work by Arteta to find Berg . . . on now to Nerlinger . . . into the penalty area . . . Nerlinger shoots . . . Howard stops it . . . and it fell to a red shirt. That could have gone anywhere but it fell in Manchester United's fortune. And here's Quinton Fortune . . . he's tackled, won back by Nerlinger, he comes forward, runs into Nicky Butt!

The pressure's building here on Manchester United . . . can they hold out and get a vital three points? It's crossed in to the penalty area . . . very high . . . O'Shea, unaware of what's going on around him, heads it away and Giggs slaps it up field. Straight to Ross for Rangers.

We're into stoppage time, I haven't seen the fourth official yet, don't know how much time's been added on . . . three, even four minutes. Here come Rangers again. Mols, just outside the United penalty area . . . and then Mols's pass back was poor . . . just kept in play on the far side by Lovenkrands . . . back to Craig Moore.

Where's the fourth official? Wakey-wakey!

SCHMEICHEL   I think he's gone to sleep!

GREEN   Where is he? Is he nodding off? We've played nearly a minute of injury time already. Rangers nil, Manchester United one, and the ball's out of play on the far side and it's a throw-in to Manchester United. There's no excuse now – either his machine – his board isn't working! Just stand out there and wave your arms . . .

BUTCHER   He's just asked Sir Alex Ferguson how long there is to go . . .

GREEN   That's the sensible thing to do . . . excuse me, Sir Alex, how much longer do you want . . ? *(Mimics Sir Alex)* . . . aye, a minute'll do, son. *(They all laugh)* We've had the minute.

Manchester United are a goal up, and, and . . . good value for it. Giggs . . . to O'Shea . . . trying to take the ball off O'Shea . . . and then O'Shea is obstructed by his former colleague Henning Berg and it's a free kick to Manchester United. A relieving free kick and I can only assume there's something wrong with the board. Have we all missed it?

BUTCHER   Yup.

GREEN   Three minutes, we think. Which is what I thought it would be . . . but no confirmation. We've played nearly two of those three minutes, if it really is three minutes. Keane with a sensible free kick . . . it's played back to Fortune, keeping possession for United.

Forward to Giggs. Giggs, down the left hand side, teasing Maurice Ross, plays it in now, takes the return pass from O'Shea.

Giggs, going forward, tackled by Ricksen, the ball's deep inside the Rangers half. It needs to be further forward for those in blue. It's clipped forward for Mols, Mols takes it on his chest . . . back it goes to Arteta . . . in to Berg . . . inside the centre circle. Poor ball by Berg, easily intercepted by Gary Neville.

Gary Neville runs down the left hand side, van Nistelrooy's ahead of him . . . and it's played to the Dutchman and there are about thirty seconds to go.

Van Nistelrooy can keep it in the far corner, very contentedly.

Well, a Rangers player went in to challenge, bounced off van Nistelrooy as if he's half dead, and anyway the ball's out of play for a throw-in to Manchester United. And here's, um, the diplomatic time-wasting substitution from Sir Alex.

Djemba – Djemba's coming on and that'll take up another thirty seconds. Strictly speaking, of course, thirty seconds should be added on for the substitution. How many referees actually adhere to that rule I do not know . . . but Djemba – Djemba for Quinton Fortune, who, you know, I saw him limp off against Leeds on Saturday morning Peter, and I wouldn't have given anything for Fortune's chances of playing tonight but he has played and he's played really well.

SCHMEICHEL Yes, absolutely right, nobody gave him a chance to play this game, he's started the game and he's been absolutely awesome. He's sat in midfield just protecting the back four and he's supported the front players whenever he's been called upon and he's just been awesome, you know, looking at him on Saturday morning and seeing him today you just can't believe it's the same player.

GREEN Yes, I agree.

BUTCHER You can definitely say, Alan, that he's stamped his mark on this game.

GREEN Oh, yes, we won't forget his stamp. But he's also unrecognisable as the player I first saw. I didn't think he had enough to make it at a club with the stature of Manchester United but Fortune is a key member of this squad now and usually a key member of the team.

Finally the throw-in is taken. We've had our, we've had four minutes of stoppage time now. The ball is played back with Klos . . . one last attack for Rangers, that's all it can be.

It's an under-arm ball out from the goalkeeper to Ross . . . in to Berg . . . Berg's made an awful hash of it . . . Paul Scholes picks it up . . . Scholes forward . . . edge of the penalty area . . . around Berg, Berg brings him down, that has to be a penalty! What a laugh! The referee's not given a penalty kick for a clear foul!

SCHMEICHEL Yeah, well, I don't want to start anything, I'll let you two say whatever –

GREEN Well, it's just a ridiculous decision . . . absolutely laughable . . .

BUTCHER A farce, absolute farce!

GREEN Hah!

BUTCHER Scholes goes inside Berg quite comfortably, Berg sticks his leg out, Scholes goes down, that's it!

GREEN Well, it's as well for Manchester United that the final whistle has gone now, because if Rangers had got an equaliser suddenly, well, there would have been all sorts of mayhem after that ridiculous cop-out by the referee.

Roy Keane and Gary Neville are going up . . . so too is van Nistelrooy towards the referee . . . this is a shocking, mind-blowing decision not to give a penalty kick but it does not affect the result. Rangers have lost to Manchester United!

In this extract the conventions of radio commentary are used to good effect by the Radio Five commentators, Alan Green, Peter Schmeichel and Terry Butcher. For example, you will notice their use of non-standard English which increases the immediacy, excitement and tension of the commentary, especially at the end of such an important game.

1 The conventions used by the commentators are listed in column 1 of the table below.

Note down further examples of these conventions in column 2. Then explain how these contribute to the game's atmosphere in column 3.

Radio commentary techniques	Evidence	How this contributes to the atmosphere of the game
Use of dramatic pause	good work by Arteta to find Berg . . . on now to Nerlinger . . . in to the penalty area	
Mixture of past and present tense	Howard stops it . . . and it fell to a red shirt	The pause between past and present here increases the feeling of anticipation for the listener as we wait the commentator to make the link between the two and satisfy our interest.
Short, snappy sentences	in to Berg . . . Berg's made an awful hash of it . . . Paul Scholes picks it up . . . Scholes forward . . . edge of the penalty area . . .	

Radio commentary techniques	Evidence	How this contributes to the atmosphere of the game
Use of humour	*(Mimics Sir Alex)* . . . aye, a minute'll do, son. *(They all laugh)*	
Imagery	The pressure's building	Use of personification here helps the listening public to visualise the intensity.

2 The purpose of radio commentary is to act as the 'eyes' of the radio audience. In this sense the commentary explains, describes and narrates, as well as informing and entertaining the audience. Use the events described in this extract to produce a newspaper report on the match. Below is a possible opening for the article, with brief details of the preceding action.

Remember to include:

- your own headline for the article (some examples have been given below)
- a continuation of the article in the same style
- invented quotes from the two managers on their side's performance – Alex McLeish (Rangers); Alex Ferguson (Manchester United).

FERGIE THE SMARTER ALEC

NEVILLE SILENCE BOOBOYS WITH DEADLY STRIKE

NEVILLE MIND ALEX

Glasgow Rangers 0 Manchester United 1

Goal-shy Phil Neville plunged Rangers into greater despair last night after scoring the winner in the so-called Battle of Britain. The unlikely hero, Phil Neville, hadn't scored a European goal since November 1998 when he contributed to the 5–0 Old Trafford rout of Brondby.

And it was the result of a 40-yard mazy run that mesmerised the Rangers rearguard and left the Scottish champions reeling. After only five minutes had passed, the passionate Ibrox crowd was stunned into silence.

A newspaper article should:

- include a dramatic headline to capture reader's attention
- sum up the story's main points of interest in its opening paragraph
- develop the story
- use supporting evidence
- include personal responses to what occurred
- include facts
- use some emotive vocabulary.

D2: Live Interview with Will Smith

Introduction

BBC Radio One began broadcasting in 1967 and marked a conscious effort to target younger listeners who had become dissatisfied with BBC Radio's output and had turned to **pirate radio stations** during the 1960s. Radio One has traditionally been dominated by the popular music charts and to a large extent this is still the case. However, a recent trend in the media is the increasing overlap, or **synergy**, between the music, film, television, publishing and radio industries. Radio One has reflected this in the way that it feeds its listeners on a diet drawn from all areas of **popular culture**, and not just the music chart.

The following extract is an example of a celebrity interview. It was broadcast on Sarah Cox's *Breakfast Show* and features Radio One's film correspondent, James King, chatting to Will Smith. The interview is a good example of synergy between the radio and film industries. Radio One gain a five minute interview with an **A-list** Hollywood film star and Columbia Pictures gain a great opportunity to publicise their new film, *Men in Black 2*.

Number of parts: 2
Parts in order of appearance:

James King
Will Smith

Live Interview with Will Smith

JAMES   Hi Will. How you doing? You good?

WILL   What's the deal baby?

JAMES   You feeling good?

WILL   Man, listen. Life is gravy right now.

JAMES   Life is gravy is it?

WILL   Life is gravy yeah.

JAMES   That's a word I don't know.

WILL   You like that one?

JAMES   That means good?

WILL   You know, gravy like you have potatoes, mashed potatoes and you put gravy on the mashed potatoes. It means like you've got everything you need. And the gravy is just extra. Life is gravy, man.

JAMES   And its gravy because of *Men in Black 2*?

WILL   Well, you know, that's a good part of the gravy. It opened real well in the States. And people are laughing in the movie theatres. So that's always a good thing.

JAMES   And that suit. You're back in the black suit. How does it feel to slip that back on after, what has it been, five years now?

WILL   Yeah. It was a little tight when I first put it on, as I was coming off of *Ali* and I was a little bigger than when I made the last film. But no, it felt good, man, getting back. It's like, you know, family coming back together, you know – the director, and the co-stars. When you're making a sequel its like coming back together more than when you start a film, its really you're getting to know people and it's a slow start and all that. We really kind of hit the ground running.

JAMES   It's not exactly the same suit though is it. They haven't kept it in storage for that . . .

WILL   Oh no, no, no, no. But they'll generally, you know. They'll start it with the same measurements, which was a bad idea.

JAMES   So, what was more difficult then, putting on weight for *Ali* or losing it for *Men in Black 2*?

WILL   Putting on the weight was much more difficult. Any change in your body is gonna be, you know, really equally difficult, putting on weight or losing weight. There's a certain zone that your body wants to stay in so any change you have to make a drastic change in your life. So it was definitely harder putting it on. I lost eleven pounds in one day!

JAMES   How did you do that?

WILL   Well, it was in Africa and I was in the ring outside for sixteen hours – boxing. So the weight will definitely fall off you.

JAMES   You're back, as you said, with your co-star from the first movie, Tommy Lee Jones.

WILL   Yeah.

JAMES   Now, I'll be honest with you. I've never met Tommy Lee Jones but I do find him quite scary. And you say in this movie how he never smiles because he doesn't smile in this movie. And he is for me quite an intimidating figure. I hope that you're gonna tell me that he is a laugh and a joker and a very nice guy.

WILL   Yeah. He's definitely a very nice guy. But with Tommy and the Press it's the first question, man. That's the one that you've got to get. You've got to nail the first question. You know it has to be no questions to start with . . . So what's it like? . . . or . . . So how was it? . . . None of those. None of those, you know. Tommy graduated from Harvard, you know what I mean? So it's like he's a borderline genius. You've got to come at him right. So, get your questions, man, you ready? Don't be scared.

JAMES I'm slightly scared still but I'll do my best. Also in the movie some new characters pop up in Part 2. Notably, there's a very funny cameo. Now, some people may know about it already but I don't want to give the game away. Let's just say there is a cameo in it from someone who's probably the most famous person of, say, the last thirty years.

WILL Yeah. Easily, easily.

JAMES Let's tease a bit. How does it happen and what does he do?

WILL Well, he called Steven Spielberg and Barry Sonnenfeld and myself and he said he just loved the first movie and if there was ever a Part 2 that he had to be in it. So, when he heard there was gonna be a Part 2 he started calling again and said 'put me in this movie'. So, he's there. He has his black suit on and he's very funny. The little cameo is very funny.

Activities: Live Interview with Will Smith

Radio One is marketed mainly to a young audience who want to be entertained and informed by radio programmes. In this interview, James King matches the style and language of his questions both to his audience and to the interviewee, Will Smith.

1   In pairs, identify one example of where listeners are informed and one where they are entertained in this interview. Make notes in a table like the one below, using the examples to guide you.

Inform	Entertain
JAMES So, what was more difficult then, putting on weight for *Ali* or losing it for *Men in Black 2*? WILL Putting on the weight was much more difficult.	JAMES You feeling good? WILL Man, listen. Life is gravy right now. JAMES Life is gravy is it? WILL Life is gravy yeah.

2   The entertainment is provided by the way that Will Smith uses words cleverly to reveal his thoughts on his current and past film career.

a)   Explain how the extended metaphor of 'gravy' is used.

b)   Imagine that Will Smith's film career has been terrible recently and *Men in Black 2* was a disaster at the box office. Choose a new metaphor which you think will best describe this situation. For example 'nose dive'.

c)   You have won a competition to interview your favourite celebrity. Produce ten questions which you would like to ask him/her. Do not ask closed questions, i.e. questions that only require a Yes/No answer.

For example, don't ask:

> 'Did you enjoy shooting the video?'
> Do ask:
> 'Describe what it was like shooting the video.'

3 You have been given the chance to write a 15-minute slot for Radio One's Breakfast Show. In groups of four, plan what you are going to write. Include some of the following:

- selection of music
- interview with a music/sport/film star
- quizzes
- phone-ins
- competitions
- film reviews
- music reviews
- news headlines.

You may wish to use a grid like the one below to plan your 15-minute slot.

Time	My commentary	Guests/Phone-in/ News reporters	Music/Sound effects

Make sure that the content of your 15-minute slot is varied, informative and entertaining. In order for your writing to fit the needs of a teenage audience, you must consider the following:

- when introducing a particular music track, it's not enough to say, 'And here's Jennifer Lopez'. Give background information about the song and artist as well as commenting on why you like or dislike the track
- for competitions and phone-ins, choose topics and prizes that will be suitable for the needs of your teenage audience
- for news and sports bulletins, remember to make them concise.

Section E: Funny Bones

E1: Only Fools and Horses

Introduction

Only Fools and Horses is a situation comedy, or sitcom, that ran on the BBC from 1981 until 1997. It featured two brothers, Del and Rodney Trotter, and an older relative, initially their Grandad and later their Uncle Albert.

The extract here was written as a short special for BBC Comic Relief in 1997. Despite being made after the final Christmas trilogy, it is set before the Trotters became millionaires.

Del and his girlfriend Raquel have a son called Damien who Del thinks could become a model. However, Rodney can't help thinking of him as the baby (called Damien) who was possessed by the devil in the horror film *The Omen*.

Number of parts: 5
Parts in order of appearance:

Rodney
Damien *(doesn't speak)*
Albert
Del
Raquel

Only Fools and Horses

Scene. Int. Del's flat (living room), Nelson Mandela House.

> *Rodney is sitting at the table, eating pizza and reading holiday brochures. Damien is sitting in the corner, next to Albert, also eating pizza. Albert is sitting on his chair, listening to the stereo. Del enters from kitchen, and hands Rodney a can of beer.*

DEL Here you go, Rodders. *(Turns to Damien)* Alright, champ? *(Cut to Damien, smiling. Cut back to Del, looking over Rodney's shoulder.)* Oh! Thinking of taking Cassandra away on a little holiday to Greece, are you?

RODNEY Thinking being the operative word.

DEL That's very near the place that I went about four years ago. 'Orrible, it was. Cor dear, yeah. Mosquitoes the size of sparrows – showed up on radar. And the place we stayed at – cor, dear – the room was never swept, the food was diabolical, and the sheets, they weren't changed from one week to the next.

RODNEY You should have gone self-catering.

DEL We did. And then, of course, the little one, he went and got a tummy bug, dashing to the **khazi** every five minutes.

RODNEY Yeah, alright – I get the picture!

DEL And then Raquel was frightened that Damien might catch it. *(Rodney looks at Albert and Damien, puzzled.)* So, when are you thinking of booking your holiday then?

RODNEY Del, we're not going to book the holiday. Me and Cass sat down last night and worked out our finances.

DEL Well, what's happened to your wages?

RODNEY My wages?! I usually blow them on a doner kebab on the way home!

DEL	No, I meant your combined wages, didn't I? I mean, Cassandra, like, she earns well, doesn't she?
RODNEY	We've gotta pay the mortgage on our flat, the loan on Cassie's car, rates, life insurance, pensions, heating, food and clothing.
DEL	That's what I mean – you waste it! Listen to me, though. I had a thought last week.
RODNEY	Oh, you should have said something – we'd have had a little celebration!
DEL	Don't you get **sarky** with me, Rodney! This financial situation ain't all my doing. But I have thought of a way of bringing some serious money in. Modelling.
RODNEY	*(surprised)* Modelling?
DEL	Yes, yes! Photographic modelling. Clothes, you know, that sort of thing for magazines and maybe – what – even the telly? *(Rodney points to himself and then Del.)* Hmm? No, not us two you dipstick! Him! *(Points over to the corner of the room, where Albert and Damien are sitting.)*
RODNEY	Albert?
DEL	Oh, for god's sake! What could that old duffer be – Captain Birdseye's stunt man?
RODNEY	Well, who then?
DEL	Damien!

Cut to Damien, covered in pizza, and smiling sweetly. Cut back to Rodney, with an alarmed look on his face.

RODNEY	Oh, I don't think that's a very good idea, Del.
DEL	Why not? He's a good looking kid and these model agencies, they're desperate for little **chavvies** to do adverts like Smarties and all that. Just think Rodders, this time next year . . . his little face could be on every television set in the country.

Rodney looks over at Damien again.

RODNEY   No, no. I don't think it's right, you know, parents pushing kids into show business.

DEL   No, I wouldn't be pushing him, would I? It's in his blood. I mean, you know, look at Raquel.

RODNEY   What about her?

DEL   Well, she was in show business, weren't she?

RODNEY   She was a stripogram!

DEL   Once, Rodney! Just once.

RODNEY   What I'm trying to say is, it's unfair to force Damien to do something he might not want to do. I mean, when he's older, he might choose to take up modelling. He might even enjoy it, but it would be his decision.

DEL   You think the world of that little boy, don't ya?

RODNEY   *(wonders what to say, and then smiles.)* Well.

DEL   Yeah, I can tell that you do 'cause I can see it in your eyes! Here you are, aren't you lucky, Damie? You've got an uncle that loves you nearly as much as your mummy and daddy.

RODNEY   *(changing the subject)* So, anyway, we're still stuck in the same potless situation ain't we?

ALBERT   You two don't know when you're well off.

DEL &
RODNEY   Oh, God!

ALBERT   During the war . . .

DEL   Oh, God!

ALBERT   . . . I saw real hardship. Refugees, entire families had lost their homes and didn't know where their baby's next meal was coming from. Same thing's happening today. You think you're hard up, Rodney? Well, think about Africa.

DEL   What are you talking about? I mean, if he can't afford to go to Greece, he certainly can't afford to go to Africa!

RODNEY   No, Del. I think he means, you know, all the starving people in Africa.

DEL   Oh, yeah. Yeah, that's right. We never really think about that, do we?

RODNEY   No. Well, once a year when it comes on the telly.

DEL   I mean, well, you know, we think we're hard up but, we've got a roof over our head, ain't we? And we eat every day. It's what I've always said, Rodney. 'One man's floor is another man's ceiling'.

ALBERT   *(sadly)* We couldn't help them people back in 1941 'cause we didn't have anything ourselves, but times have changed. I'd love to be able to just open a door and walk back into 1941.

RODNEY   How can anyone just walk back to 1941? That's stupid!

RAQUEL   I'm going to bed, Del.

DEL   Yeah, alright. Goodnight, Sweetheart. *(Rodney pauses, with a strange look of deja-vu on his face.)*[1] Yeah, don't be so stupid, Albert. I'm not a Detective Inspector, but even I can work that one out![2]

---

[1] Nicholas Lyndhurst (Rodney) plays a character who travels back to 1941 by going through a door in the BBC romantic comedy series called *Goodnight Sweetheart*.

[2] David Jason (Del) plays Detective Inspector Jack Frost in the ITV police drama *A Touch of Frost*.

Activities: Only Fools and Horses

In this scene, we see how the director has used camera work cleverly to increase the comic effect. From these activities you will learn how to piece together the dialogue and action into a storyboard. You will also discover how the following techniques are used in making TV.

Camera shots

- Pan shots (camera moves from side to side from a fixed axis).

- Tilt shot (camera moves up and down from a fixed axis).

- Crane shot (camera moves around at a distance above ground level).

- Rolling shot (camera moves diagonally in a distorted way for dramatic effect).

- Close ups/long shots.

Lighting

- Low-key lighting which may be used to create a dark or sinister mood – possibly for comic and ironic effect in this scene.
- High-key lighting that may present a brightly lit room/mood.

Editing – How the action is pieced together

- A straight cut.
- A fade (a scene slowly fades to black).
- A jump cut (the audience's attention is brought into focus by a sudden cut).

1 Working in the role of Assistant Producer for this piece of TV, you are going to produce a detailed storyboard of the main action. Each frame of the storyboard should include details of camera shots, lighting and editing. Follow the guidelines below, reading the examples carefully.

a) In groups of three, as Del, Rodney and Albert, read and act out the script.

b) Decide between you how many camera shots there are in this scene. Use the plan underneath as a guide.

Camera shot	Action
1	*Camera focuses on Rodney and zooms to Damien, sitting in a corner. The camera then focuses on Albert who is eating a pizza and listening to the radio.*
2	*Del enters from the kitchen, and hands Rodney a can of beer.*

c) Next copy out the table below to produce a detailed storyboard for this script. Remember to use the language of camera shots, lighting and editing from page 97, e.g tilt shot or a fade.

Scene number	Camera shot	Lighting	Editing	Sketch	Action/ Dialogue

E2: A Bit of Fry and Laurie

Introduction

Stephen Fry and Hugh Laurie are well-known actors, writers and radio and television performers. They met at Cambridge University where they first started writing and performing together.

A Bit of Fry and Laurie was a BBC television sketch show that they co-wrote and performed for three series in the early 1990s. *We Haven't Met* is a short sketch from the third series and like many of their sketches takes a great delight in both language and the absurd through the use of puns, word play and irony.

Number of parts: 2

Parts in order of appearance:

Hugh

Stephen

A Bit of Fry and Laurie

A drinks party. Hugh approaches Stephen.

HUGH Hello. We haven't met, Terry Swale. My wife tells me that you're new to Yorkshire.

STEPHEN Yes, I'm a bit of a southerner, I'm afraid.

HUGH Whoops! Can't have that. *(Laughs)*

STEPHEN No! *(Laughs)* My mother's family came from Sheriff Hutton, though.

HUGH Ah, well perhaps there's some hope for you! *(Laughs a great deal.)*

STEPHEN *(also laughing a great deal.)* Yes!

HUGH So.

STEPHEN Ng.

Pause.

(At length) I must say everyone seems very friendly.

HUGH Well it's not all whippets and cloth-caps, you know. *(Laughs)*

STEPHEN No. No. *(Laughs)*

HUGH We have heard of avocados and hot and cold running water. *(Shrieks with laughter)*

STEPHEN *(also laughing)* Hot and cold running water! Avocados. That's lovely. So, you live . . . ?

HUGH Boroughbridge way.

STEPHEN Ah, lovely.

HUGH Well, you know. We've got the Moors handy and the Dales. Ten minutes and you can be in York, Ripon or Harrogate. We like it.

STEPHEN Right. Lots of good air and lovely walks, I should imagine.

HUGH Ye-e-s. But we have all got cars, you know.

STEPHEN   Well, naturally.

HUGH   I mean it's not all fell-walking and climbing boots.

STEPHEN   No. Right.

HUGH   You should see some of the traffic we get in Thirsk and Harrogate.

STEPHEN   Oh.

HUGH   And the pollution in Leeds can rival anything you've got down south, we like to think.

STEPHEN   Mm.

HUGH   Oh yes. Sometimes takes me two hours to get to work there are so many cars.

STEPHEN   Well, right. It can be terrible, can't it? I always used to go to work by bicycle when I was living in London.

HUGH   You can't move in Ripon for bicycles. Worst bicycle jams in Britain.

STEPHEN   Right. Still, it's a much better place to bring up the kids. I mean, quality of life and everything. Less of the seamier side of life to . . .

HUGH   We have heard of sex and violence up here, you know.

STEPHEN   Well, obviously.

HUGH   We like to think that there are more drug-related muggings, rapings and beatings in the Vale of York than anywhere outside America. See that woman over there? Sally Oldcastle. She runs the biggest crack ring in Europe. And what's more she's not stuck-up.

STEPHEN   Good Lord. So there's not much that's different from London, really.

HUGH   You said it, mate. Whatever they've got down South, there's more of up here and it's cheaper and more expensive and you can't park.

STEPHEN   Right, right. Well it's getting late, I think I'll just translocate myself home now.

HUGH	Beg pardon?
STEPHEN	I must translocate myself home with my personal translocation podule.
HUGH	What the hell's that?
STEPHEN	Well it's basically just the same as a domestic translocation podule, but you wear it on your wrist that's all.
HUGH	Yeah, what does it do?
STEPHEN	I punch in the grid coordinates of where I am now, then the coordinates of wherever it is I want to go, press the button on the side and hey presto.
HUGH	Hey presto?
STEPHEN	My molecular structure disintegrates and reassembles within a matter of seconds at my chosen destination.
HUGH	Hang on, hang on . . .
STEPHEN	What?
HUGH	You mean like *Star Trek*?
STEPHEN	I'm sorry?
HUGH	You mean you go all wobbly and then disappear?
STEPHEN	My God.
HUGH	What?
STEPHEN	You mean you've never seen one of these before?
HUGH	Er . . .
STEPHEN	They're all the rage down South. My daughter bought me this at a petrol station. It's the Sinclair version, but some of the Japanese ones are really fabulous.
HUGH	Wait a minute.
STEPHEN	What?
HUGH	If you've all got these things . . .
STEPHEN	Yes?

HUGH What do you need petrol stations for?

STEPHEN For everlasting life.

HUGH I'm sorry?

STEPHEN Everlasting life. They discovered it a couple of years ago in Southampton. If you drink a gallon of petrol every day, you'll live for ever. You must have heard that?

HUGH That? Oh yeah. We drink petrol up here, all right. Yeah. Live for ever, we do, sometimes longer.

STEPHEN Well I should hope so. I'm just amazed you don't have personal translocation podules.

HUGH Who said we don't have them?

STEPHEN Well I just thought . . .

HUGH Designed and built up here, those things. We've had 'em for years. In fact, they've come and gone.

STEPHEN Have they?

HUGH Oh yeah. They were a sort of craze for a while but nowadays . . . no, I was just surprised to see . . .

STEPHEN Oh, well would you like to have a go on mine? For old time's sake.

HUGH No thanks.

STEPHEN Sure?

HUGH I've had a couple of drinks. Don't want to get pulled by the law when my molecules are all over the place.

STEPHEN Fair enough. Well, I'll be on my way.

Stephen grabs a cloth-cap and puts it on his head. He collects a leash on the end of which there is a whippet.

HUGH What are those?

STEPHEN Cloth-cap and whippets. All the rage down South. Bye.

He presses a button on his watch and disappears.

Activities: A Bit of Fry and Laurie

In the extract word play is used cleverly to create much of the humour for the audience. Sarcasm is used heavily to reveal stereotypical views that people can have towards a particular culture or region. In this case Stephen and Hugh explore stereotypical views of people 'up North' and 'down South'. Hugh's character, in particular, is mocking the media's portrayal of Yorkshire and London.

1   Reread the script to find examples of the stereotypes that Stephen and Hugh discuss. Two examples have been done for you in the table below.

Examples of stereotypes	Who is being mocked? North or South?
HUGH Well it's not all whippets and cloth-caps, you know. *(Laughs)*	North
HUGH And the pollution in Leeds can rival anything you've got down south, we like to think.	South

2   Stereotypes can be used in a comical way but they can also lead to prejudice and discrimination, which can cause conflict between races. In groups of four, discuss the following statements:

Stereotypes in TV can lead to prejudice and discrimination
versus
Stereotypes in TV are just harmless fun.

First, plan the discussion using these stages:

• define the term 'stereotype'
• provide examples of stereotypes that you may find in TV. (For example, Kevin and Perry are stereotypically 'bad teenagers' in their dress, manners and attitude, see page 25.)
• give evidence for and against the statements
• plan your conclusion and feed back to the rest of the group.

3   This extract explores the issue of people wanting to outsmart each other. For everything that Stephen says about London, Hugh argues that Yorkshire does it far better. Hugh is defensive about Yorkshire and tries to compete with London. For example, on the issue of traffic and pollution Hugh has this to say.

> But we have all got cars, you know.
>
> You should see some of the traffic we get in Thirsk and Harrogate.
>
> Sometimes takes me two hours to get to work there are so many cars.
>
> You can't move in Ripon for bicycles. Worst bicycle jams in Britain.

Using this idea, work in pairs to produce a short comic script titled 'Mine's better than yours!'

You should base it on your area and a contrasting area so that the two characters can compete with each other. Make it ridiculous and amusing.

Write out the script and perform it to your class. Follow this example.

NEIL: Salford, now that's where you see some mint cars – I saw 5 Mercedes parked in our avenue last week.

NOEL: Yeh, well that's nothing. In Moss Side where I live, my brother's got 10 Jags.

NEIL: Well, my dad owns a Rolls Royce garage.

NOEL: So! My great granddad invented the car.

E3: Blackadder Goes Forth

Introduction

Each series of BBC's *Blackadder* featured six episodes set in a particular historical period. The format allowed for broad comedy of situation based on consistent characters like Edmund Blackadder and Baldrick. It also allowed for elements of satire which were dependent on the specific historical period being depicted. The cleverly titled fourth series of the *Blackadder* sitcom *Blackadder Goes Forth* was set in the trenches of the First World War.

Richard Curtis wrote the first series of *Blackadder*. He is one of the most successful writers for television and film of his generation. He has written *The Vicar of Dibley*, *Four Weddings and a Funeral* and *Notting Hill* as well as being the main force behind BBC's Comic Relief appeals.

The last three series of *Blackadder* were co-written with Ben Elton. He also co-wrote *The Young Ones* as well as writing *The Thin Blue Line* and appearing as a successful stand-up comedian. Ben Elton has also written several best-selling novels, stage and screenplays.

The extract is from the first episode of the fourth series. Captain Blackadder has been called from the trenches to see Colonel Melchett. He suspects that Melchett will want to send him on a highly dangerous mission. He, on the other hand, is looking for a chance to get away from the trenches and almost certain death.

Number of parts: 5
Parts in order of appearance:

Blackadder
Darling
Melchett
George
Baldrick

Blackadder Goes Forth

At staff HQ. Darling is at his desk writing. Blackadder enters.

BLACKADDER What do you want, Darling?

DARLING It's Captain Darling to you. General Melchett wants to see you about a highly important secret mission.

MELCHETT *(enters)* What's going on, Darling?

DARLING Captain Blackadder to see you sir.

MELCHETT Ah, excellent. Just a short back and sides today I think, please.

DARLING Er, that's Corporal Black, sir. Captain Blackadder is here about the other matter sir, the *(lowers his voice)* secret matter.

MELCHETT Ah, yes, the special mission. At ease Blackadder. Now, what I'm about to tell you is absolutely tip-top-secret, is that clear?

BLACKADDER It is sir.

MELCHETT Now, I've compiled a list of those with security clearance, have you got it Darling?

DARLING Yes sir.

MELCHETT Read it please.

DARLING It's top security sir, I think that's all the Captain needs to know.

MELCHETT Nonsense! Let's hear the list in full!

DARLING Very well sir. 'List of personnel cleared for mission Gainsborough, as dictated by General C. H. Melchett: You and me, Darling, obviously. Field Marshal Haig, Field Marshal Haig's wife, all Field Marshal Haig's wife's friends, their families, their families' servants, their families' servants' tennis

	partners, and some chap I bumped into the mess the other day called Bérnard.'
MELCHETT	So, it's maximum security, is that clear?
BLACKADDER	Quite so sir, only myself and the rest of the English-speaking world is to know.
MELCHETT	Good man. Now, Field Marshal Haig has formulated a brilliant tactical plan to ensure final victory in the field. *(They gather around a model of the battlefield.)*
BLACKADDER	Now, would this brilliant plan involve us climbing out of our trenches and walking slowly towards the enemy sir?
DARLING	How can you possibly know that, Blackadder? It's classified information.
BLACKADDER	It's the same plan that we used last time, and the seventeen times before that.
MELCHETT	E-E-Exactly! And that is what's so brilliant about it! We will catch the watchful Hun totally off guard! Doing precisely what we have done eighteen times before is exactly the last thing they'll expect us to do this time! There is however one small problem.
BLACKADDER	That everyone always gets slaughtered in the first ten seconds.
MELCHETT	That's right! And Field Marshal Haig is worried that this may be depressing the men a tad. So, he's looking to find a way to cheer them up.
BLACKADDER	Well, his resignation and suicide would seem an obvious solution.
MELCHETT	Interesting thought. Make a note of it, Darling! Take a look at this: 'King & Country'.
BLACKADDER	Ah, yes, without question my favourite magazine; soft, strong and thoroughly absorbent.

MELCHETT	**Top-hole** Blackadder, I thought it would be right up your alley. Now, Field Marshal Haig's plan is this; to commission a man to do an especially stirring painting for the cover of the next issue, so as to really inspire the men for the final push. What I want you to do, Blackadder, is to labour night and day to find a first rate artist from amongst your men.
BLACKADDER	Impossible sir. I know from long experience that my men have all the artistic talent of a cluster of colourblind hedgehogs . . . in a bag.
MELCHETT	Hm, well that's a bit of a blow. We needed a man to leave the trenches immediately.
BLACKADDER	Leave the trenches?
MELCHETT	Yes.
BLACKADDER	Yes I wonder if you've enjoyed, as I have sir, that marvellous painting in the National Portrait Gallery, 'Bag Interior', by the colourblind hedgehog workshop of Sienna.
DARLING	I'm sorry, are you saying you can find this man?
BLACKADDER	I think I can. And might I suggest sir that having left the trenches, it might be a good idea to post our man to Paris *(points on Melchett's map)*, in order to soak up a little of the artistic atmosphere. Perhaps even Tahiti *(points)*, so as to produce a real masterpiece.
MELCHETT	Yes, yes, but can you find the man?!
BLACKADDER	Now I know I can sir. Before you say 'Sunflowers' I'll have Vincent van Gogh standing before you.
	Back in the trenches. Blackadder is painting, George is looking over his shoulder.
GEORGE	No, don't stop sir. It's coming, it's definitely coming. I, hm, yeah, ah, er, hm. I just wonder if two

socks and a hand-grenade is really the sort of thing that covers of 'King & Country' are made of.

BLACKADDER They will be when I paint them being shoved up the Kaiser's backside.

George walks over to Baldrick.

GEORGE Ah, now, now this is interesting.

BLACKADDER What is?

GEORGE Well, Private Baldrick is obviously some kind of an impressionist.

BLACKADDER The only impression he can do is of a man with no talent. What's it called Baldrick? 'The Vomiting Cavalier'?

GEORGE That's not supposed to be vomit; it's dabs of light.

BALDRICK No, it's vomit.

GEORGE Yes, now er, why did you choose that?

BALDRICK You told me to sir.

GEORGE Did I?

BALDRICK Yeah, you told me to paint whatever comes from within, so I did my breakfast. Look, there's a little tomato.

BLACKADDER Hopeless. If only I'd paid attention in nursery art-class instead of spending my entire time manufacturing papier-mache willies to frighten Sarah Wallis.

GEORGE You know it's funny, but painting was the only thing I was ever any good at.

BLACKADDER Well, it's a pity you didn't keep it up.

GEORGE Well, as a matter of fact I did, actually. I mean *(takes out pictures)* I mean normally I hadn't thought I would show them to anyone, because they're just embarrassing daubs really, but you know, ah, they

	give me pleasure. I'm embarrassed to show them to you now as it happens, but there you go, for what they're worth. To be honest, I should have my hands cut off, I mean . . .
BLACKADDER	George! These are brilliant! Why didn't you tell us about these before?
GEORGE	Well you know, one doesn't want to blow one's own trumpet.
BLACKADDER	You might at least have told us you had a trumpet. These paintings could spell my way out of the trenches.
GEORGE	Yours?
BLACKADDER	That's right, ours. All you have to do is paint something heroic to appeal to the simple-minded Tommy. Over to you Baldrick.
BALDRICK	How about a noble Tommy, standing with a look of horror and disgust over the body of a murdered nun, what's been done over by a nasty old German.
GEORGE	Excellent. I, I can see it now; 'The Nun and the Hun'.
BLACKADDER	Brilliant! No time to lose. George, set up your easel, Baldrick and I will pose. This is going to be art's greatest moment since Mona Lisa sat down and told Leonardo da Vinci she was in a slightly odd mood. Baldrick, you lie down in the mud and be the nun.
BALDRICK	I'm not lying down there, it's all wet.
BLACKADDER	Well, let's put it this way; either you lie down and get wet, or you're knocked down and get a broken nose.
BALDRICK	Actually it's not that wet, is it?
BLACKADDER	No. *(Pushes Baldrick down, splat.)*
BALDRICK	Who are you going to be then sir? The noble Tommy?

BLACKADDER	Precisely, standing over the body of the ravaged nun.
BALDRICK	I want a wimple.
BLACKADDER	You should have gone before we started the picture.
BALDRICK	You know, the funny thing is, my father was a nun.
BLACKADDER	*(firmly)* No he wasn't.
BALDRICK	He was so, sir. I know, 'cos whenever he was up in court, and the judge used to say 'occupation', he'd say 'nun'.

George enters, dressed in painter's smock and hat, carrying a palette and easel.

BLACKADDER	Right. *(To George)* You're ready?
GEORGE	Just about sir, yes. Erm, if you just like to pop your clothes on the stool.
BLACKADDER	I'm sorry?
GEORGE	Just pop your clothes on the stool over there.
BLACKADDER	You mean, you want me . . . tackle out?
GEORGE	Well, I would prefer so sir, yes.
BLACKADDER	If I can remind you of the realities of battle, George, one of the first things that everyone notices is that all the protagonists have got their clothes on. Neither we, nor the Hun, favour fighting our battles '**au naturel**'.
GEORGE	Sir, it's artistic licence. It's willing suspension of disbelief.
BLACKADDER	Well, I'm not having anyone staring in disbelief at my willie suspension. Now, get on and paint the . . . thing, sharpish!

Activities: Blackadder Goes Forth

This extract shows how humour can be created effectively through the medium of television. The serious topic of war is ridiculed through a clever use of language and sarcasm that the characters enjoy. This leaves the audience with a sense that they should at no point take the action too seriously. The success of these two scenes is a result of:

- comic timing
- humorous dialogue
- use of puns
- the way the characters interact with each other
- exaggeration
- juxtaposition (where two or more sections are put together for dramatic effect).

Much of the comedy derives from the writers mocking the media's portrayal of the war as being heroic, through tales of glory and victory. The writers satirise the war by mocking its seriousness.

1   Below are four examples of comic moments from the extract. First, identify why these extracts are humorous by circling particular lines and noting the technique used. Then explain what aspect of the war is being mocked.

Remember to refer back to the techniques list above. The first example has been done for you.

Extract	Explanation of why the scene is humorous
DARLING Very well sir. 'List of personnel cleared for mission Gainsborough, as dictated by General C. H. Melchett: You and me, Darling, obviously. Field Marshal Haig, Field Marshal	Exaggerated titles and overuse of military language is mocking the army and their obsession for titles and status.

Extract	Explanation of why the scene is humorous
Haig's wife, all Field Marshal Haig's wife's friends, their families, their families' servants, their families' servants' tennis partners, and some chap I bumped into the mess the other day called Bérnard.' MELCHETT So, it's maximum security, is that clear? BLACKADDER Quite so sir, only myself and the rest of the English speaking world is to know.	Use of exaggeration. Mocking the notion of top security by giving a ridiculous number of people clearance. The idea of maximum security is cleverly put next to this list for dramatic effect (juxtaposition). This is again mocking the notion of 'top secret' by basically saying everyone will know yet we will claim it is top secret.
Captain Blackadder to see you sir. MELCHETT Ah, excellent. Just a short back and sides today I think, please. DARLING Er, that's Corporal Black, sir. Captain Blackadder is here about the other matter sir, the (*lowers his voice*) secret matter.	
MELCHETT Good man. Now, Field Marshal Haig has formulated a brilliant tactical plan to ensure final victory in the field. (*They gather around a model of the battlefield.*)	

Extract	Explanation of why the scene is humorous
BLACKADDER Now, would this brilliant plan involve us climbing out of our trenches and walking slowly towards the enemy sir? DARLING How can you possibly know that Blackadder? It's classified information.	
BLACKADDER That everyone always gets slaughtered in the first ten seconds. MELCHETT That's right! And Field Marshal Haig is worried that this may be depressing the men a tad. So he's looking to find a way to cheer them up. BLACKADDER Well, his resignation and suicide would seem an obvious solution.	

2   In pairs, write the next scene for this script where Blackadder, along with Baldrick, brings the painting to Darling as his passport out of the trenches. Include lines for the following characters:

- Blackadder
- Darling
- Baldrick
- Melchett.

  ꞁꞁꞁ ꞁ ꞁose of this script is to entertain and amuse your audience. Use the techniques listed above to create an original and humorous script. Your playscript should last about 2 minutes.

Section F: Conflict in Childhood

F1: Kes

Introduction

This script is a film adaptation of the novel *A Kestrel for a Knave*. Both the novel and the screenplay were written by Barry Hines. The film was directed by Ken Loach and starred David Bradley, Brian Glover, Lynne Perrie and Colin Welland.

Kes is the story of a fifteen-year old boy, Billy Casper, who lives in a northern coal- mining town. His father has left home and he lives with his mother, who ignores him, and his half-brother Jud, who pushes him around. Billy is no good at school and has been in trouble with the police. He is about to leave school and will have to go to work in the local pit, which he really does not want to do. His life is a hard one, particularly at school, where he is bullied by his classmates and by some of the teachers. A fight is bound to happen sooner or later . . .

Number of parts: 5
Parts in order of appearance:

Billy
Friend (doesn't speak)
MacDowall
Mr Farthing
Kids
Boys (*don't speak*)
Crowd *(doesn't speak)*

Kes

Sequence 27. Playtime. The fight on the coke.

The playground is full. BILLY wanders around – perhaps he is with another lad, the left-back whom he talked to during the games lesson. He walks round to the corner – like the cycle sheds – some BOYS are smoking, some keeping watch. They include MACDOWALL.

MACDOWALL   Got owt, Casper?

BILLY hasn' t.

MACDOWALL   You never have, you just cadge all the time. Casper the cadger, that's what they ought to call thee.

BILLY   I wouldn't give thee owt if I had, MacDowall.

MACDOWALL   I'll give thee summat in a minute.

BILLY and FRIEND walk away.

MACDOWALL   What's tha' gone over there for, Casper, frightened? What's up, don't you like company? They say your mother does –

I've heard you've got more uncles than any kid in this city.

The other BOYS' reaction.

BILLY   Shut your mouth.

MACDOWALL   Come and make me.

BILLY   You wouldn't say that to our Jud. He'd murder thee.

MACDOWALL   Would he heck, he's nowt your Jud.

BILLY   You what! He's cock of the estate, that's all.

MACDOWALL   Who says? I bet I know somebody who could fight him.

BILLY   Who? Thi father?

The OTHERS laugh and begin to separate from MACDOWALL.

MACDOWALL   Your Jud wouldn't stick up for thee anyroad, he isn't even your brother.

BILLY   What is he then, my sister?

MACDOWALL   He's not your right brother, my mother says. They don't even call him Casper for a start.

BILLY   Course he's my brother! We live in the same house, don't we?

MACDOWALL   And he don't look a bit like thee, he's twice as big for a start, you're nowt like brothers.

BILLY runs at him, shouting that he's going to tell Jud what MacDowall's said.

MACDOWALL pushes BILLY off with his foot, and as BILLY comes back he punches him hard which sends him flying back on a heap.

MACDOWALL   Get away, you little squirt, before I spit on you and drown you.

BILLY goes to the pile of coke nearby, and hurls coke at MacDowall. MACDOWALL calling threats at Billy, backs up towards him, and as BILLY pauses to pick up more lumps, runs up the coke towards him. As BILLY tries to run further up the pile, his feet sink into the coke, and MACDOWALL catches him up. They fight on the coke.

From all over the playground KIDS come running, calling out 'Fight, Fight'.

The CROWD pushes in all round the edge of the coke, scrunching it up, spreading it out.

MACDOWALL seems to be winning the fight on the coke but it is a hard struggle.

MR FARTHING appears and pushes his way through the crowd. As they see him, BOYS move off and the CROWD melt away. When he reaches the centre of attraction he lifts MACDOWALL off Billy and turns to the other Lads.

FARTHING   I'm giving you lot ten seconds to get back round to the yard. If I see one face after that time I'll give its owner the biggest belting he's ever received.

He starts to count. After a few seconds only MACDOWALL and BILLY remain. Then he asks them what's going on: they don't reply at once, so he asks Billy again.

BILLY   It was him, sir! He started it.

MACDOWALL   I didn't sir! It was him he started chucking cokes at me.

Allegations and counter allegations what for though – nowt – you liar, etc.

FARTHING   Shut up, both of you. It's the same old tale, it's nobody's fault and nobody started it, you just happened to be fighting on top of a heap of coke for no reason at all.

Just look at the mess you've made. Just look at it! It's disgusting.

And look at the state of you both.

Don't look so sorry for yourself Casper, you're not dead yet.

MACDOWALL   He will be when I get hold of him.

FARTHING   You're a brave lad aren't you, MacDowall? He's just about your size, Casper, isn't he? Well if you're so keen on fighting why don't you pick on somebody your own size, eh? Eh?

During this MR FARTHING jabs MACDOWALL in the shoulder, and as MACDOWALL backs away, he walks after him, punctuating his speech with jabs.

They have moved back into the bicycle shed.

FARTHING   What would you say if I pinned you to the floor and smacked you across the face?

You'd say I was a bully, wouldn't you lad? And you'd be right because I'm bigger and stronger, and I know I could beat you to pulp before we started. Just like you know, MacDowall, with every boy you pick on.

MACDOWALL's spirit is now well and truly broken.

MACDOWALL   I'll tell my dad.

FARTHING   Of course you will lad. And then do you know what I'll do, MacDowall? I'll tell mine. And then what will happen? Eh?

MACDOWALL's head bangs on the bin at the back of the shed.

FARTHING   And do you know, MacDowall, that my dad's the heavyweight champion of the world? So what's going to happen to your dad then, eh? And what's going to happen to you, eh, eh MacDowall?

Farthing has won.

FARTHING   Well what's it like to be bullied? You don't like it much do you? Well you'll like it even less if I ever catch you at it again. Understand?

MACDOWALL says he does.

FARTHING   Right, you'd better start shovelling that lot back into place. Get on with it lad.

FARTHING turns to Billy.

FARTHING   Now then Casper, what's it all about?

Activities: Kes

In this extract the issue of bullying is presented to the audience in a powerful and direct way. The victim, Billy, is picked on because of his impoverished appearance and small size. He is an easy target for the bullies yet on this occasion decides to fight back, and gains an unlikely ally in his teacher, Mr Farthing.

1 The director of the film manages to create sympathy for Billy. Three of the techniques he uses are listed in the table below. Find examples in the script and explain how they create sympathy and support for Billy's plight. An example of each technique has been completed for you.

Techniques	Evidence	How this helps to create sympathy and support for Billy.
Director's notes	*BILLY wanders around – perhaps he is with another lad . . .*	The use of the word 'wanders' creates the idea that Billy is lost and lonely in his world.
Use of dialogue	What's up, don't you like company? They say your mother does – I've heard you've got more uncles than any kid in this city.	The cruel jibe by MacDowall helps to reflect Billy's miserable home-life. It further reinforcing the picture of him being neglected.
The role of Mr Farthing	Well if you're so keen on fighting why don't you pick on somebody your own size, eh? Eh?	Mr Farthing turns the tables on the bully, helping to support Billy.

2   This film adaptation of *A Kestrel for a Knave* is very effective in presenting the themes of family life, education and bullying. In this extract the writer's own views on these topics come through strongly. In a small group, discuss what you believe the writer's views are on these themes.

You may wish to use this plan to guide your discussion.

Themes	Writer's views	Evidence from text	Your own views
Family life			
Education			
Bullying			

3   Imagine you were a witness to both the fight and Mr Farthing's confrontation with MacDowall. Write an eyewitness account of the events. This is a piece of recount writing, so the text should be in the past tense and events should be described in a powerful and emotive way.

Remember to include:

- details of the fight
- comments on Mr Farthing's role
- descriptions of how the characters involved must have felt at each point. You may wish to include words such as: humiliated (Billy); ashamed and frightened (MacDowall); proud and angry (Mr Farthing)
- your character's thoughts and feelings about the event.

F2: The Full Monty

Introduction

The Full Monty became the most successful British film ever after its release in 1997. This success was in large part thanks to the backing the film received from Hollywood distributors Fox Searchlight. However, it was also due to the way in which Simon Beaufoy's script touched a nerve with both male and female audiences. The film is a comedy, but has serious things to say about important aspects of social change in Britain. It shows a post-industrial northern community where old certainties about work and family no longer hold true.

In the chosen extract Gaz, the unemployed father of Nathan, tries to book a club for his newly formed group of male strippers. He cannot let the club-owner know what the booking is for and finds he needs £100 deposit. He has no money. He wouldn't have resorted to male stripping if he did. Deciding to swallow his pride Gaz tries to borrow the money from Mandy, who is his ex-wife and Nathan's Mum.

Number of parts: 12
Parts in order of appearance:

Gaz
Nathan
Alan
Mandy
Cashier *(doesn't speak)*
Gerald *(doesn't speak)*
Dave *(doesn't speak)*
Lomper
Guy
Horse *(doesn't speak)*
Sheryl
Louise *(doesn't speak)*

The Full Monty

Ext. Working men's club. Day.

GAZ and NATHAN are remonstrating with Alan, the gnarly owner of the working men's club. ALAN never once breaks his steady rhythm of loading crates of beer from the street into the club.

GAZ Come on, Al, it's me.

ALAN And that's precisely why it's a hundred quid up front. Half price. You book me club for nowt, you don't turn up – give me back word – and I'm left with an empty bar on a Saturday night. No can do, kid.

GAZ 'Course we'll turn up. Al, I haven't got a hundred quid . . .

ALAN stops loading crates and looks Gaz in the face.

ALAN If you tell me what you're up to it might help.

GAZ *(after a long pause)* I can't. Top secret.

ALAN Sorry, youth.

Int. Factory. Day.

On the shop floor, MANDY is overseeing a line of women who are automatically snapping the arms of plastic dolls into their torsos. She spots NATHAN and GAZ gesturing over the noise of the machines and the radio. She goes over to them and ruffles Nathan's hair.

MANDY Hiya love. *(To Gaz)* What do you want?

GAZ Hiya, Mandy, y'alright? Listen, I'm going to get all your money for you – our money – Nathan's – oh you know what I mean. For definite this time.

MANDY Right, yeah. That all?

GAZ Thing is, Mand, you have to give out to get back, don't you? In business, like.

MANDY I'm not sure I'm hearing this.

GAZ I'll get it all – the whole lot. I just need –

MANDY – you want some money? I need someone in' packing section. It's two fifty an hour. You can start now. You coming?

GAZ can' t even try to explain. MANDY turns on her heel and walks back to the assembly line.

Int. Building society. Day.

NATHAN drags Gaz by the hand into the building society.

GAZ Nathan, you can't do this, it's your savings, kiddo.

NATHAN can barely see over the till.

NATHAN I can. I just need your signature, don't I? It says in' book. *(To the cashier)* I'd like to take me money out please.

GAZ Well, you can't have it. *(To the cashier)* You're alright, love, it's sorted.

NATHAN It's my money. I want it. A hundred pounds, please.

GAZ Well, when you're eighteen you can walk in here and get it yourself, can't you?

NATHAN You said you'd get it back.

GAZ *(reasoning)* I know, but you don't want to listen to what I say.

NATHAN You *said* so. I believe you.

GAZ You do?

NATHAN Yes.

GAZ Blimey, Nath.

The CASHIER looks at Nathan and Gaz, stamps Nathan's book, counts out a hundred pounds and slides it across to Nathan. NATHAN solemnly gives it to Gaz.

Ext. Sheffield Street. Day.

The GANG are walking casually down the street. GAZ looks around and nods his head. Suddenly, GERALD whisks a bucket out from under his parka, DAVE slops the wall-paper paste on a hoarding, whilst LOMPER slaps up a poster advertising Hot Metal's first appearance. GUY and the HORSE lean casually either side to block the view.

GUY It's not straight.

LOMPER Give over. It's only a poster.

Down the street come SHERYL and LOUISE. High-heeled and dangerous, they know Gaz of old.

GAZ Aye up, gents. This is all we need. Alright, sweethearts?

SHERYL Garry the lad. What you up to then, Shifty?

GAZ Bit o' this, bit o' that, bit o' the other.

LOUISE snatches a poster from under Lomper's coat and eyes it archly.

Just a bit of advertising. For some mates, like.

SHERYL *(not buying it for a second)* Oh aye? And whose gonna want to see your 'mates'? We had the real thing up 'ere t'other day.

GAZ *(disconcerted)* Well, we – us mates, are better.

SHERYL And how's that then?

GAZ *(searching for inspiration)* Well . . . er, this lot go all the way. *(Big smile)* Don't they, lads?

Activities: The Full Monty

This extract presents a series of images reflecting working-class culture. Although the film is set in Sheffield, it could be based in any town or city. The director is able to create the gritty humour of Northern life through the selection of exchanges and the character's use of slang. There are four settings in this particular extract that are shown below.

1   In the following boxes, find examples of the character's use of slang. Some have been done for you.

Scene	Slang used
Working Men's Club	quid
Factory	y'alright?
Building society	it's sorted
Street	Aye up

2   Using this language, and any appropriate slang words you may know, write and perform a dramatic monologue from one of the characters below:

   • Gaz
   • Nathan
   • Mandy.

   (A dramatic monologue is a speech delivered by an actor alone on stage. It is used to reveal the character's innermost feelings.)

   You could start in the following way:

   Gaz: Feel terrible that our Nath's got that dough from the bank. His mam'll kill us if she finds out.

3   In this film, 'the show' that the characters put on at the club involves them stripping off as a way of earning money. From the

extract it is clear that Mandy, Gaz's ex-partner, does not know about their radical idea.

Write the scene where Mandy finds out from Nathan that his dad has not only taken £100 quid from his savings, but plans to use it to help him fund the show. The following characters will take part:

- Gaz
- Nathan
- Mandy.

Make the scene tense but most of all funny and entertaining for the audience. You could start like this:

MANDY: You've done what!!??

(Mandy picks up the frying pan as Gaz retreats behind Nathan.)

GAZ: Listen love, I can explain. Nathan, tell y'mam about this.

Remember to include the following in your script:

- brief director's notes
- dialogue which reflects their speech in the existing script
- descriptions of the set
- each character's body language.

F3: East is East

Introduction

East is East is a British film that was released in 1999. It had started life as a successful stage play written by Ayub Khan-Din. The setting is Salford, Lancashire, in 1971 and the story revolves around the Khan family. Pakistani father, George, and white mother, Ella, run the local chip shop and struggle to cope with their seven children. *East is East* is about what happens when two cultures collide within one family, but it is also written in the tradition of northern working-class comedy.

The following extract deals with the recurring source of conflict within the Khan family. Arranged marriages, a traditional and vital part of the Muslim way of life for George, are for his children a symbol of the cultural void between them and their father.

In this scene we see the struggles and pressures that Nazir faces on the day of a marriage that has been arranged by his father.

Number of parts: 23
Parts in order of appearance:

Kids (*don't speak*)
Crowd (*doesn't speak*)
Tariq (*doesn't speak*)
Saleem (*doesn't speak*)
Maneer (*doesn't speak*)
Meenah
Sajid (*doesn't speak*)
Ella (*doesn't speak*)
Auntie Annie (*doesn't speak*)
Poppah Khalid (*doesn't speak*)
Mr Moorhouse
Stella Moorhouse

Earnest Moorhouse
Nazir
George
Abdul
Women (*don't speak*)
Men (*don't speak*)
Iyaaz Ali Khan
Mullah (*doesn't speak*)
Bride's Family (*doesn't speak*)
Bride
Man (*doesn't speak*)

East is East

16. Ext. Khan's house.

*The front door of the Khans' house opens and out
come the KIDS. A CROWD of onlookers throw confetti
and rice over them. First comes TARIQ then, SALEEM,
MANEER, MEENAH, SAJID and ELLA. A neighbour's
dog sniffs at Meenah's sari as she passes, and receives
a kick from MEENAH which makes it whelp. They all
pile into a brightly painted mini-bus which is decorated
with tinsel, silver paper and ribbons.*

*AUNTIE ANNIE, mid-fifties, Ella's best friend is
standing by the mini-bus talking to POPPAH KHALID, a
Pakistani in his mid-thirties.*

*Across the street, standing on his doorstep watching,
is MR MOORHOUSE, in his late fifties, and a look of
distaste on his face, his hair is short and white. Besides
him, stands his granddaughter STELLA MOORHOUSE, a
pretty girl of eighteen. She watches Tariq Khan intently.*

MR MOORHOUSE   Look at that, a piccaninny's picnic.

*STELLA says nothing, but we can see that she finds this
upsetting. She catches Tariq's attention and gives him
a little smile. MR MOORHOUSE sees it.*

MR MOORHOUSE   Who are you grinning at?

STELLA   No one Grandad . . . they just look funny
that's all.

*EARNEST MOORHOUSE, 12, Sajid's friend, is on the
floor scraping up the used confetti. He is scruffily
dressed in an old baggy jumper and dirty old plimsolls
with the fronts flapping. He wears blue National Health
glasses that have a Band-Aid across one lens.*

EARNEST   You look lovely, Meenah.

MEENAH   Get stuffed, Pongo.

Suddenly he notices NAZIR being led out by GEORGE and ABDUL. EARNEST is completely mesmerised by the sight. The CROWD 'oohs' and 'ahhs' and there is a storm of confetti as NAZIR passes by.

POPPAH KHALID slams on an eight track of Pakistani wedding music. The sound of drums and the shehnai (Indian recorder) fills the street. The mini-bus moves off in a shower of confetti and rice; the CROWD parts and watches the mini-bus go off down the street.

17. Int. Church hall. Rochdale.

We're now in a large church hall with trestle tables covered in soft drinks and boxes of crisps. It has been divided into two definite sections, men on one side, women on the other, the only common denominator being the infants running around and playing games. ELLA is sat amongst the WOMEN, looking completely out of place in her two-piece skirt and jacket, smoking a cigarette. MEENAH is sat next to her, equally out of place in her sari, as all the other women wear shalwar khameez. There is a small stage on which NAZIR sits with ABDUL and SAJID.

GEORGE beams with pride as MEN congratulate him. IYAAZ ALI KHAN, a slick suited man in his mid-to-late-thirties, smoking a cigar, is keeping the other Khans entertained. He looks like a film star. The ceremony has not taken place yet, people are still waiting for the Mullah. IYAAZ ALI KHAN goes over to the stage.

NAZIR   What's happening?

IYAAZ ALI KHAN   Mullah was on nights at the mill, must have overslept.

The door to the hall bursts open and the MULLAH hurries in with two or three other MEN. He shakes out an umbrella and heads for the stage. All the MEN assemble round Nazir. From another door comes the BRIDE'S PROCESSION. A figure dressed in brilliant red and gold, the BRIDE weeps on her Mother's shoulder, as do the other WOMEN who surround her. A MAN behind her throws change in the air, and the CHILDREN rush around trying to get it. Eventually they make it up to the stage, and she is sat by Nazir's side. Her veil is lifted and we see a stunningly beautiful girl. TARIQ sits up and takes notice as soon as he sees her. ABDUL helps GEORGE part Nazir's tinsel veil. NAZIR suddenly stands and looks straight at George.

GEORGE   You alright son?

NAZIR starts to pull away, trying to say something to George but it won't come out.

ABDUL   What's wrong our kid?

ELLA hears the commotion and looks up, she knows something is wrong.

GEORGE   Come son, sit down, everything OK.

The BRIDE'S FAMILY is now looking over, concerned at the delay. The MULLAH is looking at George questioningly. GEORGE goes towards Nazir, NAZIR backs away from George; he pulls off his turban and diadem and lets them fall to the ground, the tears leaving a long black line from the kohl on his eyes.

GEORGE   Sit down, no do this.

NAZIR   I'm sorry, Dad.

*GEORGE grabs Nazir and slaps him. **BEAT**. MEN move in.*

NAZIR suddenly bolts for the door, knocking over a table as he does. A scream goes up from the BRIDE'S FAMILY, people start to shout. ELLA runs for Nazir but he's too quick and is out of the door before she can get to him. GEORGE cries out to him.

GEORGE   Naziiiiir!

NAZIR bursts through the door of the hall, wind and rain come into the hall from the open doors. A terrible silence. EVERYONE looks at George. The other KHANS look on in disbelief; we see how deeply humiliated GEORGE is. He runs towards the open doors, holding the tinsel veil Nazir threw to the ground.

18. Ext. Church Hall.

We see GEORGE framed in the doorway, lashed by the wind and rain, the tinselled veil a wet mess in his hands.

19. Int. Khans' parlour.

Caption: Six Months Later

On the wall we see the photographs of Ella and George and surrounding them in order of age, are the pictures of the Kids. There is a blank space where Nazir's has been removed.

Activities: East is East

1   The opening section consists of stage directions which help to set
    the scene for the actors, cameramen/women and director. The
    conflict between cultures is firmly set in the opening exchange
    between Mr Moorhouse and Stella.

    a) Describe in your own words Mr Moorhouse's attitude towards
        the Asian people in this scene.

    b) In pairs, discuss and prepare a three-minute formal
        presentation on the topic: 'Being caught between two
        cultures'. You may wish to refer to a similar occasion where
        either yourself or a friend has been a victim of prejudice or has
        been caught between two groups of people who expect
        different things from you.

2   Stage directions must be brief and concise. They are written to help
    the actors establish the action and the personality of their characters.
    In fiction, a writer can present a character's feelings through the
    narrative, but in film, the actor does this for the audience.

    In column 3 of the table below, note down how each character
    must be feeling. Then in column 4, give advice to the actor on how
    they should communicate these feelings to the audience. One
    example of each has been completed.

Character	Stage direction	How the characters are really feeling	How these feelings should be communicated
Stella	STELLA says nothing, but we can see that she finds this upsetting.	She is disgusted and embarrassed at her grandad yet has come to expect it. She feels guilty that she does not confront him over his prejudice.	

Character	Stage direction	How the characters are really feeling	How these feelings should be communicated
Nazir	*NAZIR starts to pull away, trying to say something to George but it won't come out.*		You should keep your eyes fixed on your father, piercing him with every step as you move away from him. You know this will probably be the last time you will ever see him.
George	*We see GEORGE framed in the doorway, lashed by the wind and rain, the tinselled veil a wet mess in his hands.*		

3   Explain why the photograph of Nazir is not hanging in the Khans' parlour six months later.

4   In groups of four, write and perform a script which creates the scene after the failed wedding. You need to take on the roles of George and three other family members.

Remember to include the following:

- stage directions
- heated discussions of Nazir's actions (some family members may sympathise with Nazir and confront George)
- the removal of the photograph
- the realisation that Nazir is not coming back
- how George is going to deal with his humiliation.

Section G: What on Earth?

G1: The Hitchhiker's Guide to the Galaxy

Introduction

The Hitchhiker's Guide to the Galaxy, written by Douglas Adams, was first broadcast on Radio 4 in March 1978. It later became a TV series.

The following extract is from the first episode, titled *Mostly Harmless*. A man called Arthur Dent is worried that his house is about to be knocked down by the council to make way for a bypass. He receives a visit from his friend Ford Prefect. Arthur does not know that Ford is a visitor from another planet. Ford tells him that the Earth is about to be destroyed to make way for a hyperspace bypass. Arthur is forced to leave Earth and journey across the Galaxy with Ford. He visits many different planets and meets as many different life-forms. Ford's job is to gather information for the book *The Hitchhiker's Guide to the Galaxy*.

Number of parts: 4
Parts in order of appearance:

Arthur
Ford
Vogon Captain
The Book

ARTHUR WHAT'S THAT?!

FORD Arthur, quick, over here!

ARTHUR What is it?

FORD It's a fleet of flying saucers, what do you think it is? Quick, you've got to get hold of this rod!

ARTHUR What do you mean, 'flying saucers'?

FORD Just that! It's a Vogon constructor fleet!

ARTHUR A what?

FORD A Vogon constructor fleet! I picked up news of their arrival a few hours ago on my sub-etha radio!

ARTHUR Ford, I don't think I can cope with any more of this, I think I'll just go and have a little lie down somewhere!

FORD No, just stay here, keep calm, and just take hold of this . . .

VOGON CAPTAIN People of Earth, your attention please. This is Prostetnic Vogon Jeltz of the galactic hyperspace planning council. As you are no doubt aware, the plans for the development of the outlying regions of the western spiral arm of the galaxy require the building of a hyperspace express route through your star system. And, regrettably, your planet is one of those scheduled for demolition. The process will take slightly less than two of your Earth minutes. Thank you very much.

VOGON CAPTAIN There's no point in acting all surprised about it! All the planning charts and demolition orders have been on display at your local planning department in Alpha Centauri for fifty of your Earth years, so you've had plenty of time to launch any formal complaints, but it's far too late to start making a fuss about it now!

VOGON CAPTAIN   What do you mean you've never been to Alpha Centauri? Oh, for heavens sake, mankind, it's only four light-years away, you know! I'm sorry, but if you can't be bothered to take an interest in local affairs, that's your own lookout. Energise the demolition beams! I've no sympathy at all!

We hear the sound of the beams warming up, firing, and finally destroying the Earth. Then silence.

FORD   I brought some peanuts.

ARTHUR   What?

FORD   If you've never been through a matter transference beam before, you've probably lost some salt and protein. The beam should've cushioned your system a bit. How are you feeling?

ARTHUR   Like a military academy. Bits of me keep on passing out. If I asked you where we were, would I regret it?

FORD   We're safe.

ARTHUR   Oh, good.

FORD   We're in a small galley cabin in one of the spaceships of the Vogon constructor fleet.

ARTHUR   Ah. This is obviously some strange usage of the word 'safe' that I wasn't previously aware of.

FORD   I'll have a look for the light.

ARTHUR   Alright. How did we get here?

FORD   We hitched a lift.

ARTHUR   Excuse me, are you are you trying to tell me that we just stuck out our thumbs, and some bug-eyed monster stuck his head out and said 'Hi

---

	fellows, hop right in, I can take you as far as the Basingstoke roundabout'?
FORD	Well, the thumb's an electronic sub-etha device, the roundabout's at Barnard's star, six light-years away, but otherwise, that's more or less right!
ARTHUR	And the bug-eyed monster?
FORD	It's green, yes.
ARTHUR	Fine. When can I go home?
FORD	You can't. Ah, I found the light.

A sort of beepy noise is heard to mark that the lights are switched on.

ARTHUR	Good grief! Is this really the interior of a flying saucer?
FORD	It certainly is. What do you think?
ARTHUR	Well, it's a bit squalid, isn't it?
FORD	What did you expect?
ARTHUR	Well, I don't know . . . gleaming control panels, flashing lights, computer screens . . . not old mattresses!
FORD	These are the Dentrassi sleeping quarters.
ARTHUR	I thought you said they were called Vogons or something!
FORD	The Vogons run the ship, the Dentrassi are the cooks. They let us on board.
ARTHUR	I'm confused.
FORD	Here, have a look at this.
ARTHUR	What is it?
FORD	The Hitchhiker's Guide to the Galaxy. It's a sort of electronic book. It'll tell you everything you want to know. That's its job.

ARTHUR   I like the cover. 'Don't Panic'. It's the first helpful or intelligible thing anybody said to me all day.

FORD   That's why it sells so well. Here, press this button, and the screen will give you the index. You've got several million entries, so fast-wind through the index to V. There you are, Vogon Constructor Fleets. Enter that code on the tabulator, and read what it says.

The books makes a noise, stunningly similar to those made by R2-D2 in Star Wars, *when the code is entered.*

THE BOOK   Vogon Constructor Fleets. Here is what to do if you want to get a lift from a Vogon: Forget it. They're one of the most unpleasant races in the galaxy. Not actually evil, but bad tempered, bureaucratic, vicious and callous. They wouldn't even lift a finger to save their own grandmothers from the Ravenous Bug-Blatter Beast of Traal, without orders signed in triplicate, sent in, sent back, queried, lost, found, subjected to public inquiry, lost again, and finally buried in soft peat for three months and recycled as firelighters. The best way to get a drink out of a Vogon is stick your finger down his throat, and the best way to irritate him is to feed his grandmother to the Ravenous Bug-Blatter Beast of Traal.

ARTHUR   What a strange book.

Activities: The Hitchhiker's Guide to the Galaxy

In this episode a comparison is made between the Council's need to demolish Arthur's house for a bypass and the need to demolish Earth for a hyperspace bypass. The writer mocks the notion of the domineering council by making a comparison with aliens 'bypassing' Earth to make an express route through the star system. The Vogon Captain's speech to Earth has many hallmarks of the type of speech that a local councillor might make to justify bypassing a village.

1 In the table below, change the speech by the Vogon Captain into one by a local councillor from your area. Some ideas have been provided as a guide.

Vogon Captain	Local Councillor
People of Earth, your attention please.	Ladies and Gentleman of our council, your attention please.
This is Prostetnic Vogon Jeltz of the galactic hyperspace planning council. As you are no doubt aware, the plans for the development of the outlying regions of the western spiral arm of the galaxy require the building of a hyperspace express route through your star system.	
And, regrettably, your planet is one of those scheduled for demolition.	It is with deepest regret that this bypass is necessary to alleviate traffic congestion through our local village.
The process will take slightly less than two of your Earth minutes. Thank you very much.	

2 The Vogon Captain makes three speeches to earth without reply. The listeners need to imagine what the responses of the public would be.

a) In groups of four, discuss the likely response to each speech.

b) Complete the table below. One possible response to the first Vogon speech has been done. Remember that the style and tone of your writing should be light-hearted – the listener should know not to take it too seriously.

Vogon Captain	Likely response from 'Earthlings'
And, regrettably, your planet is one of those scheduled for demolition. The process will take slightly less than two of your Earth minutes. Thank you very much.	*Demolition? You've gotta be joking, sunshine. Haven't had chance to get out Matrix Revolutions yet and you're thinking about blowing the place up. Get real, Vogon.*
There's no point in acting all surprised about it! . . . . . . so you've had plenty of time to launch any formal complaints, but it's far too late to start making a fuss about it now!	
I'm sorry, but if you can't be bothered to take an interest in local affairs, that's your own lookout. Energise the demolition beams! I've no sympathy at all!	

3 The writer uses vocabulary which mocks the language of the
   science fiction genre, with words like the ones in the box below.
   Using this vocabulary and your own comical scientific terms, write
   a diary entry for Arthur describing the day he leaves Earth with
   Ford Prefect.

flying saucer
Vogon constructor fleet
sub-etha radio
galactic hyperspace
Alpha Centauri
energise the demolition beams

G2: FX

Introduction

FX was written by the poet and writer, Roger McGough.

Roger McGough is a former teacher who became a poet in the 1960s. He was one of the Liverpool Poets and a member of the pop group Scaffold during a time when the Mersey Sound dominated the British music scene. He has published 38 books, and 16 of his stage plays have been produced as well as numerous film, television and radio scripts.

McGough performs his poetry throughout the world and has established a huge television audience through his works for children, including *Sky in the Pie* and *The Great Smile Robbery*. The chosen extract is from a play McGough wrote for BBC Radio 4. It demonstrates very well how poets write in order for their words to be heard rather than read.

Number of parts: 5
Parts in order of appearance:

Narrator
Toby Farnham
Female trainee 1
Male trainee 1
Instructor

FX

NARRATOR Toby Farnham crouched over the wheel of his brand new Porsche. He was not enjoying the ride. Visibility was down to a few yards, as the fog arched its back against the windscreen like a fat, grey weasel.

Outside, a distant church clock chimed midnight, but the only sound he could hear was the steady hum of his finely-tuned engine, and the incessant swish of the windscreen wipers.

TOBY I'll never make London at this rate. What a fool I've been. I should have left hours earlier.

NARRATOR In an attempt to dispel his gloom Toby switched on the car radio. His mind drifted, as it so often did, towards Suzanne. There would be just the two of them this weekend – the country cottage, a roaring fire, champagne, and Suzanne. He whistled now, almost contentedly.

Suddenly, and without warning, the car spluttered to a halt. He cursed softly to himself. Running out of petrol at this time of night in filthy weather in the middle of nowhere – what foul luck! He switched off the ignition, the windscreen wipers, and the radio.

Rather than sit all night imprisoned in his car, he decided to brave the elements for a while in the hope of finding a garage, even a farmhouse, anything. He took a deep breath, and got out.

The fog leapt upon him, its paws on his shoulders, clinging to him, pushing its cold tongue into his nose and ears. He stumbled on, blindly. What a **pea souper**! The only sounds he could hear were his muffled footsteps and the occasional hoot of a distant owl.

He was just on the point of giving up and resigning himself to a lonely night in the car when, straight ahead, he could dimly make out the blurred outline of a building. Too big for a farmhouse – manor house, more like, even some sort of church. No lights on anywhere. He groped along the outside, looking for an entrance. He found it, a heavy wooden door, slightly ajar. Putting his left shoulder to it, he pushed, and pushed. It creaked slowly open. He was in, just in time, as the door clanked shut behind him.

Strangely, there was no handle on the inside.

It was pitch black, and wherever he was, he was locked in. He cursed softly to himself. Unable to see anything in the eerie blackness, he shuffled forward like a blindfolded two-year-old wearing his father's shoes. His left shoulder brushed against something cold and hard.

Then he heard it. The laughter, cruel, blood-curdling. He turned around, and, as he did, collided into what seemed like a coffin. A werewolf howled.

He turned and ran. Footsteps echoed after him. Thunder rumbled all around. The wind roared. He crashed into the wall. There could be no escape. In his mind's eye he saw The Thing coming towards him, half-man, half-beast. Panic-stricken, he dug his finger nails into the wall. A headless rider on a fiery horse galloped into view, followed by a horde of Indians, hotly pursued by the fourteenth cavalry. The 7.55 from St Pancras, dead on time, rattled through.

Hands over his ears, he screamed . . .

TOBY   Stop! *Stop!* STOP!!!

NARRATOR   *(pause)* And that was how they found him next morning. *(Pause)* Dead. *(Pause)* In the sound effects department of Broadcasting House.

Cut to the sound effects studio. Fade in to the sounds of a small group of BBC radio TRAINEES clapping appreciatively

FEMALE TRAINEE 1   That was brilliant.

MALE TRAINEE 1   It was great.

INSTRUCTOR   *(laughing, pleased with himself.)* Yes, well that was a bit of nonsense, put together by one of our sound engineers. A bit over the top of course, but a reminder perhaps of what can be done in a studio with a few old tapes and some BBC sound effects records.

Activities: FX

In this extract for radio we see how the use of language, combined with sound effects, helps to create a dark and sinister atmosphere – this helps the audience to imagine how the characters must be feeling. The settings are described effectively in this scene to help develop the mood, as well as variation in sentence structure.

1   The techniques that Roger McGough has used to create the powerful atmosphere in his script are listed in column 1 of the table below. Some examples have been filled in to help you. Add further examples of each technique.

Techniques	Examples
Personification Similes	*The fog arched its back against the windscreen like a fat grey weasel.*
Sounds	*Outside, a distant church clock chimed midnight . . .*
Long, complex sentences to create the mood of calm.	*There would be just the two of them this weekend – the country cottage, a roaring fire, champagne, and Suzanne.*
Shorter, more dramatic sentences to create a tense mood.	*Then he heard it.*
Description of settings	*Too big for a farmhouse – manor house, more like, even some sort of church. No lights on anywhere.*
Description of character's feelings	*He'd never make London at this rate. 'What a fool I've been,' he muttered to himself. 'I should have left hours earlier.'*

2 Using the same techniques as Roger McGough, produce a short piece of descriptive writing, titled *Being Followed*. Make sure that your readers are kept on the edge of their seats by your use of the dramatic techniques.

3 By the end of this extract, the audience has a strong sense that it should not take this piece too seriously.

   a) In pairs, read *FX* again, identifying examples of where the audience begins to feel that the extract is becoming too far-fetched.

   b) Using this idea, produce a three-minute drama script based on a scene, which seems tense and exciting at first, but then becomes increasingly difficult for the audience to take seriously.

H1: The Royle Family

Introduction

The Royle Family was an award-winning BBC comedy which mixed the elements of a sitcom (the stereotypical family, the single set, half-hour episodes with little plot development and comedy of situation rather than jokes); with the style of a documentary (hand-held camera, long-takes, long pauses and mundane, everyday dialogue).

The characters are northern and working class and the comedy is rooted in an affectionate mocking of everyday working-class life in modern Britain. One of the ironies of the programme is that we sit and watch the characters as they sit, watch and discuss well-known television programmes themselves.

The following extract is from the end of the last episode of Series Two, which is also the Christmas episode. The daughter, Denise, is pregnant and the family is in a state of excitement as they anticipate the imminent birth of Jim and Barbara's first grandchild.

Number of parts: 4
Parts in order of appearance:
Jim
Barbara
Denise
Dave

The Royle Family

In the living room Jim trumps and wafts it away, disgusted by the smell.

Barbara goes into the bathroom where Denise is crying. We only see her head and shoulders, but she's obviously sitting on the toilet.

DENISE Oh Mam, a load of water's came out. I think my waters have broken – and Dave's not even here.

BARBARA Oh Denise! Oh my God, Denise! Oh Denise. Oh love. Wait there – I'll go and ring Dave on the mobile.

DENISE Yeah. Yeah. Yeah. *I've* got the mobile.

BARBARA Oh God, Denise. Well I'll go and ring the hospital and I'll send your dad up. Jim!

DENISE Yeah, yeah.

BARBARA Jim!

DENISE Mam, don't leave me.

BARBARA Jim!

Barbara runs downstairs into the living room.

BARBARA Jim, get upstairs, our Denise's waters have broken.

JIM What's broken, Barb?

BARBARA Her waters. Get upstairs and calm her down. She's all upset 'cause Dave's not here. Here, take her this, this birthing tape, go on, the tape's already in there. Come on now.

Barbara hands Jim tape machine and tape.

JIM What is it, the *Dambusters?* And Dave would have been here only for your mother.

As Jim goes up the stairs he hums the theme to The Dambusters.

JIM	Denise it's your dad, love.
DENISE	Come in, Dad. Come in.
JIM	It's not too messy is it?
DENISE	No. Come in.

He goes in. Denise is sitting on the edge of the bath, doubled over. Jim puts the toilet seat down and sits on it, comforting his sobbing daughter.

JIM	You're all right. What's the matter?
DENISE	I don't know, I can't even remember what I'm supposed to be doing out of me baby book. I'm supposed to be doing me breathing, but I can't even remember how to breathe.
JIM	Come on, you'll be all right. Here y'are, let's play your tape eh?

Charlotte Church's Pie Jesu *plays in the background.*

DENISE	I don't know what I'm gonna do and Dave's gonna miss it and he's supposed to be helping me with me breathing and he's supposed to be counting them things – he's supposed to be counting 'em, them . . . things what I'm having. *(Really sobbing)* Dad, I'm so scared and I don't even think I want the baby anymore. And I don't think Dave wants it either – he didn't even want to feel it kicking before and I bet ya he'll leave it all to me and I don't even know anything about babies.
JIM	You'll be alright – there's nothing to it.
DENISE	What if the baby doesn't like me? What if I don't like the baby?
JIM	Of course you'll like it – you'll love it. I remember the first time when your mam put you in my arms and I looked at you, oh God you were beautiful and I knew,

I knew then, that I'd do anything for you, anything for you and our Antony.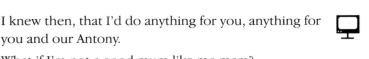

DENISE What if I'm not a good mum like me mam?

JIM You will be a wonderful mother.

DENISE Dad, if Dave don't come back, will you come with me to the hospital?

JIM Of course I will, I'll be right there outside. But your mam will be inside with you.

DENISE You promise you will, Dad? You will stay with me?

JIM Of course I'll stay with you, I'll always be there for you. Always. Ey Denise, I'm gonna be a granddad.

Barbara comes in.

BARBARA I've rang the hospital and they've told me to tell you to come in, so I've rang a taxi and it's on its way.

JIM It's double fare for Christmas Day.

BARBARA Oh Jim! Come on now, lady, let's get you downstairs.

JIM Come on, babe, let's go.

Jim and Barbara help Denise down.

BARBARA Here we go. Let me go first, love. Oh now, don't slip on this carpet, no shoes on your little feet. Are you all right?

DENISE Yeah.

BARBARA Are you hurting?

DENISE Yeah.

BARBARA It'll be over soon.

Denise cries out in pain.

BARBARA Sit down, love. Breathe, Denise. Breathe. Breathe. Good girl.

The doorbell goes.

BARBARA *(going to the door.)* Oh, let that be Dave, please let that be Dave. Oh Dave!

DAVE What's going on?

BARBARA It's all right, her waters have broken.

Barbara and Dave stand at the foot of the stairs.

DENISE Trust you not to be here when my waters broke. You're a right useless lump.

DAVE I was taking your nana home.

BARBARA It's all right Dave. Ooh Denise, Denise, you might give birth on Christmas Day!

JIM *Jesus.*

A taxi beeps its horn.

BARBARA Oh, oh, Jim, taxi. Oh, my ciggies.

Barbara goes into the living room. Dave opens the front door to shout to the driver.

DAVE Hang on a minute, pal.

JIM Right. I'll just put my shoes on.

Jim follows Barbara into the living room.

Dave (still wearing crash helmet) sits next to Denise on the stairs.

DENISE I can't believe it, Dave, it's not due for three weeks. I hope it's gonna be all right.

DAVE It will. I love you, Denise

Dave goes to give her a hug.

DENISE Oh Dave, your helmet you clown! *(She has another contraction.)* Mam! We need to go *now*. *(Dave gets up and goes.)* Dave, wait for me!

Cut to living room.

JIM *(switching off all the lights except for the Christmas tree.)* We're switching these off, I'm not made of money.

BARBARA Oh Jim. Come on, your daughter's in agony. Get your coat on.

The camera stays in the living room as Jim and Barbara go out, closing the door behind them. We see Dave, Denise, Jim and Barbara file past the living room door in silhouette (Barbara and Jim still wearing their Christmas hats).

End of Episode 7.

Activities: The Royle Family

In this Christmas episode we see Denise in the first stages of labour. Humour is created through the way that her parents, and husband Dave (eventually) react to this. All of the activities below are aimed at developing your skills in Speaking and Listening, and, in particular, Drama.

1   In groups of five, take on the roles of the Director, Jim, Barbara, Denise and Dave. You are going to act out the scene but first you must plan and prepare.

   a) Plan a storyboard – a graphic representation with a frame for each section of the script.
      This should include:

      - a brief sketch
      - notes on camera angles (close ups/long shots etc.)
      - details of sound effects
      - notes on lighting effects.

      You may wish to use the template below as a guide:

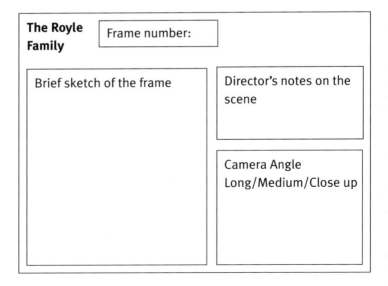

b) Your director needs to provide brief notes for each character
    on how their part should be played.
c) Rehearse the scene as a group, using the director's advice and
    the storyboard in your planning and preparation.
d) Write a critical review of your performance, analysing both
    your own and the whole group's performance.

H2: Men Behaving Badly

Introduction

Men Behaving Badly began life in the early 1990s with Martin Clunes starring alongside Harry Enfield in a peak-time sitcom **time-slot** on ITV. However, it wasn't until the programme moved to a post-**watershed** time-slot on the BBC, and Neil Morrissey replaced Harry Enfield, that *Men Behaving Badly* started to develop into a hugely popular show. The popularity of the show seemed to coincide with a trend that was recognisable elsewhere in the media that was often characterised as 'New Laddism'.

Number of parts: 6
Parts in order of appearance:

Gary
George
Anthea
Tony
Teenage Deborah
Deborah

Men Behaving Badly

8. Gary's office.

> *Late morning. Gary is sitting at his desk, still lost in thought. George is working at his desk.*

GARY George, were you there when your son was born?

GEORGE *(trying hard to remember)* No, it was a Saturday.

GARY No, not there at your desk, there at Marjorie's bedside.

GEORGE Oh, no, men didn't attend the birth in those days.

GARY Why?

GEORGE I think because the baby comes out of a lady's rude area.

GARY Ah.

GEORGE We were encouraged to go home and relax by sort of pacing. She was in labour for thirty-six hours, so I managed to pace to Reigate.

GARY So, overall, are you happy about how your son turned out, George?

GEORGE Oh, yes. Sometimes we wish he'd you know, not keep stealing our furniture and selling it, but generally we get nothing but joy from Biff.

GARY Why did you call him Biff?

GEORGE Well, he was supposed to be Bill, but the clerk at the Town Hall dropped her lunchbox on the F when she was typing the birth certificate.

GARY	So a few inches the other way, and he could have been called . . . Bipp.
GEORGE	No, that would have been silly.
GARY	I don't know – kids – what's in it for me? I'm a sexy bachelor-type person.
GEORGE	Well, doesn't it worry you that you could die tomorrow without leaving anything of lasting value?
GARY	Oh, I think you're underestimating the impact of my humorous speech to this year's Security Fencing Manufacturers' Gala.
GEORGE	The only disadvantage I can remember is that Marjorie wasn't in the mood for two years after the birth.

A pause while Gary takes this in.

GARY	Right, that's it. We're not having children.

Anthea comes in, carrying her usual bits of paper. Gary is breezy and confident again.

GARY	Anthea, remind me what's so good about being a child-free single person.
ANTHEA	Um, well, you can keep everything neat and tidy and smart around the home.
GARY	Exactly.
ANTHEA	And people don't often visit, so there's lots of time to sit and read my gardening magazines and nod off with Melody Radio on.

Gary is losing his confidence.

ANTHEA	And, of course, though I sometimes have a bit of a cry, that usually makes me feel

slightly better, and then I go mad and
have sardines on toast to really cheer
me up.

Gary gazes glumly into the middle distance.

9. Deborah's flat: Living room.

*Later that morning. Tony has made himself at
home. He is sitting on the sofa, leafing through
the last of the photo albums. He is wearing one
of Deborah's girly cardigans and sipping a vile-
coloured cocktail studded with cherries.
Bottles of spirits from her drinks cabinet are
lined up on the coffee table. He shuts the last
photo album and pours some Chartreuse into
his cocktail, turning it an even fiercer green. He
gets to his feet, surprised by the potency of the
alcohol.*

10. Bedroom.

*Tony enters, sipping his cocktail. He looks
around and grins mischievously. He puts the
glass down and jumps on to Deborah's bed.
He does an exuberant, drunken backflip, which
does not quite work. He gets off the bed and
picks up his glass again. He spies the chest of
drawers and goes over to it. He nervously looks
round, hesitates guiltily, then gingerly opens
one of the top drawers. It is a well-stocked
underwear drawer. He takes out some
expensive-looking silly knickers and wonders
what to do with them before he puts them on
his head. Delving further into the drawer, he*

finds a leather-bound book – a five-year diary. He examines it with a mixture of triumph and guilt. Agonising over whether or not to read it, he opens it an inch, then another inch, until he is reading it.

TEENAGE DEBORAH'S VOICE-OVER	Bought the Bay City Rollers' new single. I feel all funny when I think of Woody. Lisa came over, and we played it thirty-seven times. She is horrible. I hate her. She is horrible.

He throws the diary into the drawer and gets out another one. He turns to a page.

DEBORAH'S VOICE-OVER	Went to see *The Terminator* with Mike. I wanted to see *The Color Purple*. He made us sit in the cheap seats.
TONY	*(sympathetic)* Ah.
DEBORAH'S VOICE-OVER	Afterwards, feeling romantic, we went back to his place and made –

Tony stops and looks over his shoulder guiltily. He turns over the page.

DEBORAH'S VOICE-OVER	– pasta.

Tony turns to another page at the end of the diary. He reaches for his cocktail, which is on the chest of drawers.

DEBORAH'S VOICE-OVER	Tony behaved like a complete idiot today –

In surprise he knocks the full glass into the open knicker drawer.

TONY	Aaarrghh!

He jumps about, wondering what to do. In panic, he removes the drawer and empties it out on the pastel duvet, which is instantly spattered with stains. Tony stands there turning this way and that in panic.

Activities: Men Behaving Badly

In this scene the writer presents men in a comical way while mocking some people's perception that men are laddish, inconsiderate, selfish, vain and immature. In effect, the characters in the programme are stereotypes of the laddish culture often witnessed at places such as football matches or pubs. Witty dialogue, director's notes and the dramatic film device of a voice-over all contribute to the humour of the piece.

1   The table below shows the different types of humour used in the extract. In pairs, find examples of each type and note them down in column 2. Use the examples to guide you.

Type of humour	Evidence
Puns (double meaning)	GARY George, were you there when your son was born? GEORGE (*trying hard to remember*) No, it was a Saturday. GARY No, not there at your desk, there at Marjorie's bedside.
Describing a serious incident in a light-hearted, matter of fact way	
Word play and language	
Comic timing	
Exaggeration used for dramatic effect	ANTHEA And, of course, though I sometimes have a bit of a cry, that usually makes me feel slightly better, and then I go mad and have sardines on toast to really cheer me up.
Description of settings	
Description of action and movement	

2   In groups of four, rehearse and perform this scene. Use the
    dialogue and the director's notes to maximise the comic effects.
    One of you will need to 'double up' to do Deborah's voice-overs.

    - Gary
    - George
    - Anthea (could do the two voice-overs)
    - Tony

    Consider the following when performing a script:

    - position of yourself and other actors on stage
    - facial expressions
    - hand movements
    - tone of voice
    - comic timing
    - how the voice-overs are going to be used
    - props you may need, especially in the bedroom scene.

3   Using the same techniques that the writer of *Men Behaving Badly*
    uses to mock the way men are stereotyped, produce a short script
    titled 'Kids Behaving Badly'. Decide what stereotypical views
    people may have of troublesome teenagers and incorporate these
    in your script.

⊡ H3: Fawlty Towers

Introduction

Twelve episodes of the BBC sitcom *Fawlty Towers* were made between 1975 and 1979. They were written by John Cleese and Connie Booth but were inspired by an hotelier that Cleese witnessed in real life when visiting his hotel with the Monty Python team.

Each episode is a perfectly crafted descent from apparent order to complete chaos. At the centre of the chaos are the pompous, manic hotel owner, Basil Fawlty, his domineering wife Sybil, the calm and capable Polly and the hopeless but ever-hopeful waiter Manuel.

The following extract features Basil at his snobbish best. In an effort to add a touch of class to the hotel, he has hired a new chef called Kurt. However, the guests are as yet unconvinced.

Number of parts: 5
Parts in order of appearance:

Basil
The Major
Mr Heath
Mrs Heath
Ronald

Fawlty Towers

BASIL   Well, I'd better go and have a word with the guests. Why don't you have another vat of wine, dear? *(He rises and starts to circulate, coming first to the Major's table.)* Good evening, Major. Enjoying your soup?

THE MAJOR   Tasted a bit off to me, Fawlty.

BASIL   Well, it's made with *fresh* mushrooms, Major.

THE MAJOR   Ah, that would explain it.

A flicker of Olympian despair crosses Basil's face. He moves on to the Heaths' table.

BASIL   Good evening. Is everything to your satisfaction?

MR HEATH   Yes thank –

MRS HEATH   *(interrupting)* Well . . . *(She turns expectantly to their son.)*

RONALD   I don't like the chips.

BASIL   Sorry?

RONALD   The chips are awful.

BASIL   *(smiling balefully)* Oh dear. What's er. . . what's *wrong* with them, then?

RONALD   They're the wrong shape and they're just awful.

MRS HEATH   I'm afraid he gets everything cooked the way he likes it at home.

BASIL   Ah, does he, does he?

RONALD   Yes I do, and it's better than this pig's garbage.

MRS HEATH   *(slightly amused)* Now, Ronald.

RONALD   These eggs look like you just laid them.

MRS HEATH   *(ineffectually)* Ronald. . .

MR HEATH   *(to Ronald, friendlily)* Now look here, old chap. . .

MRS HEATH   Shut up!! Leave him alone! *(To Basil)* He's very clever, rather highly strung.

BASIL	Yes, yes, he should be.
RONALD	Haven't you got any *proper* chips?
BASIL	Well these *are* proper French Fried Potatoes. You see, the chef is Continental.
RONALD	Couldn't you get an English one?
MRS HEATH	*(to Ronald)* Why don't you eat just one or two, dear?
RONALD	They're the wrong shape.
BASIL	Oh dear – what shape do you usually have? Mickey Mouse shape? Smarties shape? Amphibious landing craft shape? Poke in the eye shape?
RONALD	. . .God, you're *dumb*.
MRS HEATH	Oh, now . . .
BASIL	*(controlling himself)* Is there something we can get you instead *sonny*?
RONALD	I'd like some bread and salad cream.
BASIL	. . . To *eat*? Well . . . *(pointing)* there's the bread, and there's the mayonnaise.
RONALD	I said *salad cream*, stupid.
BASIL	We don't have any salad cream. The chef made *this (indicating the mayonnaise)* freshly this morning.
RONALD	What a dump!
MR HEATH	*(offering Ronald the mayonnaise.)* This is very good.
MRS HEATH	*(coldly)* He likes salad cream.
RONALD	*(to Basil)* That's puke, that is.
BASIL	Well at least it's fresh puke.
MRS HEATH	*(shocked)* Oh dear!!
BASIL	*(indignantly)* Well, *he* said it!
MRS HEATH	*(loftily)* May I ask why you don't have proper salad cream. I mean, most restaurants . . .

BASIL Well, the chef only buys it on special occasions, you know, gourmet nights and so on, but . . . when he's got a bottle – ah! – he's a genius with it. He can unscrew the cap like **Robert Carrier**. It's a treat to watch him. *(He mimes.)* And then . . . *right* on the plate! None on the walls! Magic! He's a wizard with a tin-opener, too. He got a **Pulitzer Prize** for that. He can have the stuff in the saucepan before you can say *haute cuisine*. You name it, he'll heat it up and scrape it off the pan for you. Mind you, skill like that isn't picked up overnight. Still, I'll tell him to get some salad cream, you never know when **Henry Kissinger** is going to drop in, do you. *(Mrs Heath is silenced; Basil smiles charmingly, looks at his watch and in doing so neatly elbows Ronald in the head.)* Sorry, sorry! *(He moves off.)*

MR HEATH Nice man.

🖥 Activities: Fawlty Towers

In this extract we see the use of a comic technique titled 'farce'. Farce can be defined as . . .

> a piece of comedy which relies on a collection of ludicrous and irregular set of incidents, often leading to a series of comical exchanges.

The name of the hotel, Fawlty Towers, in itself generates connotations of silliness and humour. In this extract Basil is serving a collection of guests who are trying his patience with their excessive fussiness. The humour of this passage is created through:

- sarcasm/irony
- stage directions/character's gestures and body language
- pace of dialogue.

1. Basil is very sarcastic in this scene, both in his language and mannerisms. Identify examples of this in the script and copy out the table below to record them. Then explain the dramatic purpose of each one. One example has been completed to guide you.

Methods of humour	Evidence	Dramatic purpose
Basil's sarcasm	RONALD The chips are awful. BASIL (smiling balefully) Oh dear. What's er . . . what's wrong with them, then?	Basil is over-elaborate in his concern here which suggests he is mocking his guests and his sinister facial appearance (balefully) reinforces this sarcastic remark.
Stage directions/ character's gestures and body language	(smiling balefully) (controlling himself)	

Methods of humour	Evidence	Dramatic purpose
Speed of dialogue/ Word play	RONALD *(to Basil)* That's puke, that is. BASIL Well at least it's fresh puke.	

2 The writers of this episode have created a collection of absurd and ludicrous characters who entertain the TV audience by their eccentric mannerisms. The quick-fire exchange between Basil and Ronald in particular generates much of the humour. Working with a partner, devise a similar scenario where you are involved in a simmering yet comical exchange in a takeaway.

You could start as follows:

CUSTOMER: Aren't these supposed to be the best kebabs in Manchester? They taste like garbage!
KEBAB SHOP MANAGER: Garbage – oh yes thanks, just by the window thanks. You know so many youngsters these days just throw their rubbish on the floor.

3 Imagine you are Mrs Heath and you want to complain about the service at Fawlty Towers. Write a formal letter of complaint to the Hotel Inspectorate in which you complain about your experience at Fawlty Towers.

You may wish to refer to the examples in the table on the next page or to identify other examples in the script.

Examples of poor service	Supporting evidence from text
Food	RONALD The chips are awful. RONALD These eggs look like you just laid them.
Attitude of Basil Fawlty	MRS HEATH I'm afraid he gets everything cooked the way he likes it at home. BASIL Ah, does he, does he? RONALD They're the wrong shape. BASIL Oh dear – what shape do you usually have? Mickey Mouse shape? Smarties shape? Amphibious landing craft shape? Poke in the eye shape? (*Mrs Heath is silenced; Basil smiles charmingly, looks at his watch and in doing so neatly elbows Ronald in the head.*) Sorry, sorry! (*He moves off.*)

Section I: Passion Fruits

I1: Fever Pitch

Introduction

Four years after the publication of *Fever Pitch* the novel, came *Fever Pitch* the film: Nick Hornby himself wrote the screenplay. The film starred Colin Firth and Ruth Gemmell and was directed by David Evans.

Hornby was anxious at first about writing the screenplay as he knew it would present certain problems. Cinema is a fundamentally different medium and he would inevitably need to make changes to the book to make it work on film. The changes that he did make provide us with an interesting insight into the contrasting and complementary nature of written and cinematic expression.

The following extract from the screenplay features the same 'Home Debut' as is in the book. The central character of the boy, based on Hornby himself, is here referred to as YOUNG PAUL.

Number of parts: 14
Parts in order of appearance:

Paul	Young Paul
Steve	Arsenal Fan 1
Referee (*doesn't speak*)	Arsenal Fan 2
Steve's Brother (*doesn't speak*)	Arsenal Fan 3
Sister	Attendant
Mother	Man Behind
Father	Grumpy Supporter

> *PAUL offers Steve a cigarette. STEVE takes one, produces a lighter, lights Paul's cigarette and then his own.*

STEVE   Stanley Matthews played First Division football until he was fifty.

PAUL   I'll bet you any money you like that you're not playing First Division football when you're fifty.

STEVE   It's the smoking.

PAUL   It's not the smoking, Steve.

STEVE   PENALTY! YES!

> *The Referee is pointing to the spot. The other team protest; Steve's Brother grabs the ball and places it.*

STEVE   I've always wanted to do this.

> *He runs down the terracing, stands behind the net and starts catcalling and gesticulating at his brother. His brother runs up to take the kick, blasts it over the bar, and STEVE laughs and cheers.*

PAUL VOICE-OVER   **Anthropologists** have always had a hard time with football. The trouble is, you can only see what's on the outside. But there is an inside, believe it or not. We all have our reasons for loving things the way we do.

> *STEVE runs away as his brother chases him towards the corner flag.*

14. Flashback: Int. Young Paul's house. Day.

> *Young Paul lives in Maidenhead, some thirty miles outside London, in a quiet street full of newish Barratt*

*Home-style detached houses, each with its own
handkerchief of immaculately kept front lawn. YOUNG
PAUL is dressed up and ready to go; he is sitting on the
floor playing with his sister.*

(Teleprinter Arsenal v Stoke City, 14.9.68)

MOTHER (OOV)   He's here.

*Neither Young Paul nor his sister move. After a while
their MOTHER sweeps past them towards the front door.*

MOTHER   Thanks for being so helpful.

Their FATHER enters, dressed casually this time.

FATHER   Ready?

MOTHER   He's been ready for hours.

YOUNG PAUL   *(embarrassed)* No, I haven't.

SISTER   Yes, you have.

MOTHER   What time will you be back, do you think?

FATHER   Six, six-thirty.

MOTHER   Fine. See you later, then.

FATHER   OK.

MOTHER   Have a nice time.

He walks over to his daughter and kisses her.

FATHER   See you later, sunshine. We'll do something
special next time.

15. Flashback: Int. Car. Day.

*Young Paul and his father are in the car, driving down
the A4. The Liquidator is playing on the car radio.*

FATHER   Are you looking forward to it?

YOUNG PAUL	What?
FATHER	The football match.
YOUNG PAUL	*(unenthusiastically)* Yes.
FATHER	It sounds like it.
YOUNG PAUL	No.
FATHER	*(Slightly irritated)* One day we'll find something you do want to do.

After a pause he ruffles Young Paul's hair to show that his flash of frustration was merely good-natured teasing.

FATHER	Your mum seems in good form.
YOUNG PAUL	Yeah.
FATHER	Is she OK?
YOUNG PAUL	Not really.

The scene ends in silence.

16. Flashback: Int. Chip shot. Day.

YOUNG PAUL and his FATHER are eating a fish and chip lunch. They are sharing a table with a group of older, regular Arsenal fans, and YOUNG PAUL listens fascinated to their conversation.

ARSENAL FAN 1	What about last season?
ARSENAL FAN 2	What about it?
ARSENAL FAN 1	They were rubbish. They were rubbish.
ARSENAL FAN 2	They weren't that bad.
ARSENAL FAN 1	They were rubbish last year.

Laughter from some of the men round the table.

| ARSENAL FAN 1 | And they were rubbish the year before. And I don't care if they are top of the League, they'll be rubbish this year, too. |

More laughter.

ARSENAL FAN 1	And next year. And the year after that. I'm not joking.
ARSENAL FAN 2	I don't know why you come, Frank. Honest I don't.
ARSENAL FAN 1	Well, you live in hope, don't you?
ARSENAL FAN 3	*(to Young Paul)* What d'you reckon, old son? D'you think they're as bad as Frank says?
PAUL'S FATHER	This is his first time.
ARSENAL FAN 1	Well, I hope he knows what he's letting himself in for. Have a look at the number 8 this afternoon. Jon Sammels, his name is.

YOUNG PAUL examines his programme for the team line-ups.

| ARSENAL FAN 1 | *(continuing)* Remember his face. Then, if you should happen to bump into him, tell him to go to Spurs. |

More laughter.

17. Flashback: Ext. Street. Day.

Father and son are walking towards the stadium, past the police horses and the programme sellers and the hawkers, like other fathers and sons around them.

18. Flashback: Ext. Arsenal stadium. Day.

> *YOUNG PAUL and his FATHER walk up to a turnstile and offer their tickets to the attendant. His FATHER goes through first; YOUNG PAUL struggles with the turnstile mechanism behind him.*

ATTENDANT Go on, give it a shove.

MAN BEHIND Someone hasn't been eating their greens.

> *With a panicky shove, YOUNG PAUL makes the contraption move, to an ironic cheer from the people behind. He goes through to the stadium beyond.*

19. Flashback: Int. Stadium. Day.

> *YOUNG PAUL and his FATHER climb the wide concrete steps leading to the West Stand Upper Tier at Highbury. Again, YOUNG PAUL stares at the laughing, arguing, absorbed men as they overtake him. He reaches the top, and his FATHER examines the ticket stubs to check which block they are sitting in.*

FATHER We're in 'Q'.

> *They follow the signs, and stop briefly at the entrance to their block.*

FATHER OK?

20. Flashback: Int. Stadium. Day.

YOUNG PAUL Yeah.

> *They walk into the stand.*

21. Flashback: Ext. Stand. Day.

We see YOUNG PAUL's face as he enters a football ground for the first time; it is an intensely spiritual moment for him. For a second we cannot see what he sees; then we see Highbury – the pitch, the terraces, the stands, the thousands of people – from his point of view, and we understand, or at least sympathise. He starts to walk down the aisle, still in a dream; his FATHER, sitting just a few seats in, has to lean across and grab him, before he walks straight past. YOUNG PAUL takes his seat.

FATHER   What d'you reckon?

YOUNG PAUL   *(urgently)* When's the next game?

FATHER   I don't know. Week after next, probably. Let's have a look.

He opens the programme.

Yes. Sunderland. They're away at Leeds next week, and . . .

YOUNG PAUL   Can we come to the Sunderland game? Will you be in England?

FATHER   I don't know. We'll see. Anyway, we might want to try somewhere else. If you're going to be a football fan, you have to think carefully about who you're going to follow.

But we can tell from YOUNG PAUL's face that it is too late. Arsenal come out on to the pitch, and those in the seats around YOUNG PAUL and his FATHER stand and applaud. YOUNG PAUL, watching his neighbours carefully, follows their lead.

22. Flashback: Ext. Stand. Day.

We see YOUNG PAUL watching the game, absorbed. He does not react as the others in the crowd react; rather, he watches them watching, dumbstruck by the supporters' faces grimacing in pain, roaring, swearing, complaining and generally looking as if they are not having a good time.

GRUMPY SUPPORTER *(roaring)* You're rubbish Sammels!

23. Flashback: Ext. Stand. Day.

Arsenal score. YOUNG PAUL stands up, a little later than those around him, and cheers wildly.

YOUNG PAUL   That was a brilliant goal, wasn't it, Dad?

FATHER   Well. Pretty good, yeah.

YOUNG PAUL   What happened?

FATHER   There was a penalty, and the goalie saved it, and then there was a big scramble, and then the man who missed the penalty had another go and scored.

YOUNG PAUL   Terry Neill.

FATHER   That's right.

YOUNG PAUL   He's good, isn't he?

FATHER   *(amused)* Fantastic.

Dissolve to later in the game. All around them people are leaving their seats and making for the exits.

FATHER   Let's go.

He stands and leaves. YOUNG PAUL looks at him in disbelief, then follows.

24. Flashback: Ext. Street outside stadium. Day.

A fair part of the crowd is flooding out of the stadium and away, quiet and moderately dissatisfied. Echoing sounds of game still in progress.

YOUNG PAUL Why did we have to leave?

FATHER To beat the traffic. We've got a long way to walk back to the car, and we'll be stuck for hours.

YOUNG PAUL But they might score again.

FATHER There is a remote possibility of that, yes. But it won't be this afternoon.

YOUNG PAUL looks at his father.

FATHER Joke. And if you're going to be an Arsenal fan, you'll have to get used to jokes like that.

YOUNG PAUL *(fervently)* I will.

FATHER Who d'you think played the best?

YOUNG PAUL Dunno. *(Enthusiastically)* Sammels was rubbish, though, wasn't he?

FATHER I didn't think so. The crowd didn't understand what he was trying to do half the time. And anyway, they were on to him before he'd done anything wrong.

YOUNG PAUL I disagree.

FATHER You do, do you? One afternoon at football and you're **Kenneth Wolstenholme**.

YOUNG PAUL Who do you think played best then?

FATHER I thought Wilson was good. And I did think Sammels played well.

YOUNG PAUL He was *rubbish.*

The camera pulls away, and father and son merge back into the crowd.

Activities: Fever Pitch

1   In this extract a young boy (Paul) is introduced to football. A series
    of flashbacks reveals how Paul moves from feeling uninterested
    and intimidated to excited and absorbed by the experience of a
    live football match. This 'voyage of discovery' is presented in the
    following sequences. Imagine you are Paul and note down your
    thoughts and feelings in the table below. Use the examples to
    guide you.

Paul's voyage of discovery		
Events	Paul's likely emotions	Paul's thoughts
Waiting for Dad at home	Bored. Frustrated. Angry.	
In the car	Disinterested.	
Chip shop	Intimidated. Confused.	
Walking towards the stadium	Feels part of a family.	
Going through the turnstile		Everyone was laughing at me and dad wasn't much help. I felt a right idiot.
Entering the ground		
On the turnstile, watching the game		
Leaving the stadium		

2   In *Fever Pitch*, Nick Hornby explores the issue of obsession and
    the conflict it can cause within a family. The father is trying
    desperately to communicate to his son through football and
    eventually Paul comes to share his obsession. With a partner,
    discuss whether is a good thing to be obsessed by something. The
    plan below offers ideas to prompt your discussion.

Obsession:	
For	**Against**
Having an obsession can: • help you to socialise and get out more • give you a hobby/interest to avoid you becoming bored and getting into trouble • not prove a problem, if no one is harmed.	Having an obsession can: • make you anti-social • mean that you lose your friends • make you lose sight of what is important in life.

3   Nick Hornby uses the technique of flashback effectively in this
    extract. In this case it shows how Paul's character has developed
    over time and reveals the pressures a child can be put under.

    Choose a hobby or interest to which you are strongly committed
    and produce a plan for a short film on this aspect of your life.
    Include three flashbacks to reveal how you became involved in
    your hobby, as well as scene directions and dialogue. Use the
    table on the next page to structure your ideas.

Sequence numbers	Events	Brief director's notes explaining time/place/ characters /weather, etc.	Dialogue between characters
1	Beginning of film (present)		
2	Flashback 1 (Past)		
3	Flashback 2 Past)		
4	Flashback 3 (Past)		
5	Back to present		

I2: Secrets and Lies

Introduction

Secrets and Lies is a British comedy drama film, written and directed by Mike Leigh. As with most of Leigh's work the screenplay was developed through improvisation with a group of actors in the weeks before filming began. The story that emerged in this case was that of Hortense, a young black Londoner who goes in search of her birth mother. Hortense's journey leads her to Cynthia – a depressed, unmarried white woman living with her other grown-up daughter, Roxanne.

The following extract is from quite early in the film. Hortense's adoptive mother has died recently and her father some time before. Hortense spends time looking through her old possessions and listening to her 'family' arguing over their inheritance, before making a decision. She wants to know who her birth mother is so she can come to terms with her roots. The first step toward asserting her identity is to contact social services and seek out her birth certificate.

Number of parts: 3
Parts in order of appearance:

Receptionist
Hortense
Jenny

Secrets and Lies

> *Tuesday, HORTENSE is sitting waiting in a public building. Posters, noticeboards, a man sitting waiting along a corridor. A phone rings. A receptionist stands up into view behind a hatch.*

RECEPTIONIST   Hello?

> *A small efficient-looking WOMAN in her late thirties rushes down the stairs. She carries a shoulder-bag and a folder. She shakes Hortense by the hand.*

WOMAN   Hortense? Hallo – Jenny Ford. Nice to meet you.

HORTENSE   Oh, hi . . .

JENNY   Come this way. *(She sets off down a corridor. HORTENSE gets up and follows her.)* How are you, all right?

HORTENSE   Fine, thank you.

JENNY   Good. *(She opens a door and leads Hortense into a room at the end of the corridor.)* Sorry about this prison cell – we've been banging on about it for years, but there you go. Have a seat, make yourself at home.

> *(She closes the door. HORTENSE sits down. The room is bare and institutional. The walls are covered with notices and posters about Violence, Rights, AIDS, etc. A single toy plastic bus sits on the windowsill. JENNY sits opposite Hortense.)*

Now, before we go any further, have you got any ID? Passport, driving licence?

HORTENSE   Oh, yeah.

JENNY   You'll have to get used to all this red tape – would you like a Rolo?

HORTENSE   *(searching her bag)* No, thank you.

JENNY	Are you sure?
HORTENSE	Yeah. *(She pulls out her driving licence, and hands it over.)* There you go.

JENNY *has popped a Rolo into her mouth. She takes the licence.*

JENNY	Have a shufti . . . *(She examines it.)* That's great, Hortense. Thanks. *(She returns it.)*
HORTENSE	Thank you.
JENNY	You on your lunch break?
HORTENSE	Yeah, an extended one.
JENNY	Have you 'ad any lunch?
HORTENSE	No, not yet.
JENNY	No, me neither. So what d'you do?
HORTENSE	I'm an optometrist.
JENNY	Oh, really? Oh, God . . . *(She laughs drily)* It's one of those things you keep putting off and putting off, isn't it? *(HORTENSE smiles politely)*
	I've got to the stage with the Guardian crossword where I'm going like this. *(She demonstrates squinting)* So I think the time has come, don't you? I'll 'ave to pop in, you can give me a test. Where d'you live?
HORTENSE	Kilburn.
JENNY	Right, right. In a flat?
HORTENSE	Yes.
JENNY	D'you share?
HORTENSE	No, I live on my own.
JENNY	Oh, right. I lived on my own, for about six years – before I was married. 'T's all right, isn't it? *(She laughs)*

HORTENSE Yeah.

JENNY Right, Hortense. Let's talk a little bit about you, shall we? Now, obviously, you've been giving a great deal of thought to things, and you've come to a decision, which is good. But, for me, the question is: why now?

HORTENSE I just feel that it's the right time, that's all.

JENNY Right, right. Are you thinking about getting married?

HORTENSE No.

JENNY D'you have children?

HORTENSE No.

JENNY Are you thinking about having children?

HORTENSE *(laughing)* No.

JENNY 'T's fair enough. Are you sharing this with your parents? Do they know that you're here today? How do they feel about it?

HORTENSE They're both dead, actually.

JENNY Oh, right.

HORTENSE Er . . . Mum died . . . two months ago now . . .

JENNY Oh, that is recent – I'm sorry to hear that. Was it sudden?

HORTENSE Yeah.

JENNY Perhaps that's what's made you start on this?

HORTENSE I don't know.

JENNY It's possible.

HORTENSE Well, I'm not trying to replace her; she's irreplaceable – well, they both are.

JENNY No – of course; of course. And when you were growin' up, was it – was it a happy environment?

HORTENSE Yes, very.

JENNY	Oh, good, good, and did you, em . . . were you able to . . . to discuss the fact that you'd been –
HORTENSE	No, it was never really an issue.
JENNY	Right, right. So you've only just found out?
HORTENSE	Oh, no. They told me when I was little.
JENNY	Oh, good, good. And d'you remember how you felt about that?
HORTENSE	*(amused)* Well, it's not exactly something you forget, is it?
JENNY	No, no . . . *(returning Hortense's amusement)* I'm sure it isn't. *(Pause)* So how did you feel?
HORTENSE	Well . . . we all just got on with it as a family, d'you know what I mean?
JENNY	Yeah. Perhaps you should've discussed it.
HORTENSE	My parents loved me, and that's all that matters. Isn't it?
JENNY	Yeah, yeah. So, now that we've got you here, what are your expectations?
HORTENSE	Basically . . . I just want to know.
JENNY	Yeah, yeah – course you do. Let me share something with you, Hortense. Somewhere out there, and we don't know where, is your birth mother. Now . . . she's probably married. Perhaps not. She may have other children; she might be dead. She may even be in Australia or somewhere, we just don't know, but what we do know is . . . that, at the time she gave you up for adoption, she was under the impression that she would probably never see you again. Now, as I know you're very well aware, the law has changed since then, and you are now legally entitled to seek your birth mother out. But the snag is . . . she may not want

	to see you. So I don't want you to raise your hopes too high at this stage.
HORTENSE	Sure.
JENNY	Okay?
	HORTENSE nods.
	Have a look at this. . . *(She gives Hortense the folder.)*
HORTENSE	What is it?
JENNY	It's all about you. *(Pause)* I'll tell you what. *(She picks up her bag.)* I'll leave it with you, and I'll pop back in a few minutes. *(She gets up and touches HORTENSE gently.)* Can I get you anything?
HORTENSE	No. Thank you.
	JENNY leaves the room, closing the door behind her. HORTENSE watches her go. Then she opens the folder, and takes out a sheaf of assorted pieces of paper. She looks through them. They include some headed, 'The National Adoption Society'. She is bewildered, shocked, shaken. Tears well in her eyes.
	After a while, Jenny can be seen through a window in the door. She opens the door sensitively, but the hinges creak, and she winces as she shuts it. She joins Hortense, and for a moment rubs her back gently.
JENNY	How're you doing – all right?
	She produces a small packet of paper tissues from her bag, and holds one out for Hortense, who takes it.
HORTENSE	Thank you. *(She blows her nose.)* Cynthia Rose Purley. That's her.
JENNY	Cynthia Rose. That's a nice name, isn't it?
HORTENSE	That's her signature.

JENNY   Mm – hm. That feels strange?

HORTENSE can' t reply. Then . . .

HORTENSE   Elizabeth. That's my middle name. They must a' kept it.

JENNY   Well . . . that would be your birth name – you see: Elizabeth Purley.

(Pause. HORTENSE sighs, and wipes her nose.)

HORTENSE   Listen . . . Is there any way I could get a copy of these?

JENNY   No – those are the originals, and they're yours to keep. That's your right, under the 1975 Act – I've made copies upstairs. *(She has brought back with her a new large brown envelope, and she takes the sheaf of documents from Hortense.)* Pop those in here . . . for you. *(She does so, and swaps the envelope for the empty folder.)* So . . . what we need to do now is . . . you go away, and 'ave a think. And when the time's right, and not before – you know, it's very much in your own time . . . come back to me, if that's what you want, and we'll get the ball rolling. Now, it can be a very . . . long-winded process, and there's no two ways about it, it's a very traumatic journey we're embarkin' on; and there may be other people's feelings to consider, too. So I'll wait to hear from you, okay? Now, you could decide to trace your birth mother by yourself . . . if you wanted, but I wouldn't advise it – we're a professional service . . . *(She looks at her watch, and glances quickly over her shoulder through the window in the door.)* And we know how to handle these things. So, I think you should take advantage of us.

Activities: Secrets and Lies

In a screenplay, a director has to be concise in the descriptions of the settings and characters – partly this is because the audience can actually see the characters and places and can therefore come to their own conclusions about the events. In a novel, a writer goes into more detail to help the reader picture the scene as they cannot physically see the character's emotions and the settings described.

1   In the table like the one below, note down five pieces of director's notes, changing each into a piece of descriptive writing. Use the example to guide you.

Remember to:

- change the action from present to past tense
- be the 'eyes' and 'ears' of the reader
- use adjectives and variation in sentence structure to describe the settings and Hortense's feelings.

Director's notes from the film	Adapted from script to novel
Tuesday, Hortense is sitting waiting in a public building. Posters, notice boards, a man sitting waiting along a corridor. A phone rings.	Finally, Tuesday's daunting ordeal had arrived. Hortense sat, waiting anxiously in the intimidating and dour public building. The posters and notice boards only added to the icy feeling she had in her heart – piercing it to its deepest roots. A man was sitting in the long corridor; perhaps he too wanted the same thing – a phone call, an address, anything but this agonising wait.

2   In this meeting sequence the director builds a tense and uneasy atmosphere carefully through brief descriptions of the set, so that

the viewer identifies with Hortense's worries and apprehension. In pairs, select two examples where the director creates this tension in the script. Then note them and their effect, as shown below.

Examples of tension	Effect created on the audience
The room is bare and institutional.	*This helps the reader to identify with Hortense's increasing unease at this situation*

3 This extract deals with the issues of whether it is a good idea to try to make contact with your biological parents after you have been adopted.

a) In pairs, discuss the pros and cons of this. Feed back your ideas to the class, explaining whether you agree or disagree with Hortense.

b) Using these ideas from the discussion, produce an advice leaflet aimed at people who are considering searching for their biological parents.

Remember to include:

- the possible advantages of finding your 'natural' parents, e.g. relief, feeling of belonging, meeting some of your new family members for the first time, etc.
- the possible disadvantages, e.g. they may not wish to see you; they have a new family who do not know of you, they may live on the other side of the world.

An advice leaflet should have the following language and presentational features:

- facts and opinions
- headings/subheadings used to break up the text
- bullet points
- pictures and captions
- a friendly and supportive tone.

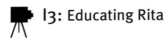 **I3: Educating Rita**

Introduction

Educating Rita was written by Willy Russell and first performed as a stage play in 1980. It was so popular that it was made into a film starring Michael Caine as Frank and Julie Walters as Rita. Willy Russell is also famous for *Our Day Out* and *Blood Brothers*.

Frank is a university lecturer who has become bored with literature, teaching, learning and his life in general. He also drinks far too much in order to relieve his boredom.

Rita is one of his Open University students, an ordinary working-class woman who has a passion to learn about books but has little formal education. Her husband Denny is not supportive of her desire to learn about English Literature; he wants her to start a family.

In the extract, Rita has just been to the theatre to see a production of *Macbeth*. She cannot wait to tell Frank how exciting and eye-opening it was for her.

Number of parts: 2
Parts in order of appearance:

Frank
Rita

Educating Rita

Scene six.

FRANK enters carrying a briefcase and a pile of essays. He goes to the filing cabinet, takes his lecture notes from the briefcase and puts them in a drawer. He takes the sandwiches and apple from his briefcase and puts them on his desk and then goes to the window desk and dumps the essays and briefcase. He switches on the radio and then sits in the swivel chair. He opens the packet of sandwiches, takes a bite and then picks up a book and starts reading.

RITA bursts through the door out of breath.

FRANK   What are you doing here? *(He looks at his watch.)* It's Thursday, you . . .

RITA   *(moving over to the desk; quickly.)* I know I shouldn't be here, it's me dinner hour, but listen, I've gorra tell someone, have y' got a few minutes, can y'spare . . . ?

FRANK   *(alarmed)* My God, what is it?

RITA   I had to come an' tell y', Frank, last night, I went to the theatre! A proper one, a professional theatre.

FRANK gets up and switches off the radio and then returns to the swivel chair.

FRANK   *(sighing)* For God's sake, you had me worried, I thought it was something serious.

RITA   No, listen, it was. I went out an' got me ticket, it was Shakespeare, I thought it was gonna be dead borin' . . .

FRANK   Then why did you go in the first place?

RITA   I wanted to find out. But listen, it wasn't borin', it was great, honest, ogh, it done me in, it was fantastic. I'm gonna do an essay on it.

FRANK *(smiling)* Come on, which one was it?

RITA moves upper right centre.

RITA '. . . Out, out, brief candle!
Life's but a walking shadow, a poor player
That struts and frets his hour upon the stage
And then is heard no more. It is a tale
Told by an idiot, full of sound and fury
Signifying nothing.'

FRANK *(deliberately)* Ah, *Romeo and Juliet*.

RITA *(moving towards Frank)* Tch. Frank! Be serious. I learnt that today from the book. *(She produces a copy of* Macbeth.*)* Look, I went out an' bought the book. Isn't it great? What I couldn't get over is how excitin' it was.

FRANK puts his feet up on the desk.

RITA Wasn't his wife a cow, eh? An' that fantastic bit where he meets Macduff an' he thinks he's all invincible. I was on the edge of me seat at that bit. I wanted to shout out an' tell Macbeth, warn him.

FRANK You didn't, did you?

RITA Nah. Y'can't do that in a theatre, can y'? It was dead good. It was a thriller.

FRANK Yes. You'll have to go and see more.

RITA I'm goin' to. *Macbeth*'s a tragedy, isn't it?

FRANK nods.

RITA Right.

RITA smiles at Frank and he smiles back at her.

Well I just – I just had to tell someone who'd understand.

FRANK I'm honoured that you chose me.

RITA *(moving towards the door.)* Well, I better get back. I've left a customer with a perm lotion. If I don't get a move on there'll be another tragedy.

FRANK No. There won't be a tragedy.

RITA There will, y'know. I know this woman; she's dead fussy. If her perm doesn't come out right there'll be blood an' guts everywhere.

FRANK Which might be quite tragic –

He throws the apple from his desk which she catches.

– but it won't be a tragedy.

RITA What?

FRANK Well – erm – look; the tragedy of the drama has nothing to do with the sort of tragic event you're talking about. Macbeth is flawed by his ambition – yes?

RITA *(going and sitting in the chair by the desk.)* Yeh. Go on. *(She starts to eat the apple.)*

FRANK Erm – it's that flaw which forces him to take the inevitable steps towards his own doom. You see?

RITA offers him the can of soft drink. He takes it and looks at it.

FRANK *(putting the can down on the desk.)* No thanks. Whereas, Rita, a woman's hair being reduced to an inch of stubble, or – or the sort of think you read in the paper that's reported as being tragic, 'Man Killed By Falling Tree', is not a tragedy.

RITA It is for the poor sod under the tree.

FRANK Yes, it's tragic, absolutely tragic. But it's not a tragedy in the way that *Macbeth* is a tragedy. Tragedy in dramatic terms is inevitable, pre-ordained. Look, now, even without ever having heard the story of *Macbeth* you wanted to shout out, to warn him and prevent him going on, didn't you? But you wouldn't have been able to stop him, would you?

RITA	No.
FRANK	Why?
RITA	They would have thrown me out the theatre.
FRANK	But what I mean is that your warning would have been ignored. He's warned in the play. But he can't go back. He still treads the path to doom. But the poor old fellow under the tree hasn't arrived there by following any inevitable steps has he?
RITA	No.
FRANK	There's no particular flaw in his character that has dictated his end. If he'd been warned of the consequences of standing beneath that particular tree he wouldn't have done it, would he? Understand?
RITA	So – so Macbeth brings it on himself?
FRANK	Yes. You see he goes blindly on and on and with every step he's spinning one more piece of thread which will eventually make up the network of his own tragedy. Do you see?
RITA	I think so. I'm not used to thinkin' like this.
FRANK	It's quite easy, Rita.
RITA	It is for you. I just thought it was a dead excitin' story. But the way you tell it you make me see all sorts of things in it. *(After a pause)* It's fun, tragedy, isn't it? *(She goes over to the window.)* All them out there, they know all about that sort of thing, don't they?
FRANK	Look, how about a proper lunch?
RITA	Lunch? *(She leaps up, grabs the copy of Macbeth, the can of drink and the apple and goes to the door.)* Me customer. She only wanted a demi-wave – she'll come out looking like a muppet. *(She comes back to the table.)* Ey' Frank listen – I was thinkin' of goin' to the art gallery tomorrow. It's me half-day off. D'y' wanna come with me?

FRANK   *(smiling)* All right.

         RITA goes to the door.

FRANK   *(looking at her)* And – look, what are you doing on
         Saturday?

RITA   I work.

FRANK   Well, when you finish work?

RITA   Dunno.

FRANK   I want you to come over to the house.

RITA   Why?

FRANK   Julia's organized a few people to come round for dinner.

RITA   An' y' want me to come? Why?

FRANK   Why do you think?

RITA   I dunno.

FRANK   Because you might enjoy it.

RITA   Oh.

FRANK   Will you come?

RITA   If y' want.

FRANK   What do you want?

RITA   All right. I'll come.

FRANK   Will you bring Denny?

RITA   I don't know if he'll come.

FRANK   Well ask him.

RITA   *(puzzled)* All right.

FRANK   What's wrong?

RITA   What shall I wear?

         Blackout.

         RITA goes out.

Activities: Educating Rita

In this screenplay, the writer includes various stage directions designed to instruct the actors how to use body language and tone of voice to reflect the character's personality. In the opening section, Frank, the University Lecturer is shown to have a relaxed attitude towards his work. For example:

> He goes to the window desk and dumps the essay and briefcase.

1   Find five other examples of stage directions in the scripts that suggest Frank has the following personality traits: Some entries have been completed for you in the table below.

Personality of Frank	Stage directions that suggest this
Relaxed	*Frank gets up and switches off the radio and then returns to the swivel chair.*
Supportive Encouraging	*Rita smiles at Frank and he smiles back at her.*

2   As activity 1 proves, stage directions are vital to the audience's understanding of characters' personalities. Taking the opening section of script, change the stage directions so that the audience gains a completely different impression of Frank's character. You only need to change the stage directions in order to create the opposite mood. The table below gives some examples in bold.

Actual script	Changed script with new stage directions
Scene Six	*Scene Six*
Frank enters carrying a briefcase and a pile of essays. He goes to the filing cabinet,	*Frank enters **lugging** a briefcase and a pile of **unwanted** essays. He goes to the filing cabinet,*

Actual script	Changed script with new stage directions
takes his lecture notes from the briefcase and puts them in a drawer. He takes the sandwiches and apple from his briefcase and puts them on his desk and then goes to the window desk and dumps the essays and briefcase. He switches on the radio and then sits in the swivel chair. He opens the packet of sandwiches, takes a bite and then picks up a book and starts reading.	*grabs his lecture notes from the briefcase and **throws** them in a drawer. He takes the sandwiches and apple from his briefcase and puts them on his desk and then goes to the window desk and dumps the essays and briefcase. He switches on the radio and then **collapses** in the swivel chair. He **rips** opens the packet of sandwiches, takes a bite and then picks up a book and starts reading.*
RITA bursts through the door out of breath	*Rita bursts through the door out of breath.*
FRANK What are you doing here? (*He looks at his watch.*) It's Thursday, you . . .	FRANK What are you doing here? (***He glares angrily** at his watch.*) It's Thursday, you . . .
RITA (*moving over to the desk; quickly*): I know I shouldn't be here, it's me dinner hour, but listen, I've gorra tell someone, have y' got a few minutes, can y'spare . . .?	
FRANK (*alarmed*): My God, what is it?	
RITA I had to come an' tell y', Frank, last night, I went to the theatre! A proper one, a professional theatre.	

Actual script	Changed script with new stage directions
Frank gets up and switches off the radio and then returns to the swivel chair.	
FRANK (*sighing*) For God's sake, you had me worried, I thought it was something serious.	
RITA No, listen, it was. I went out an' got me ticket, it was Shakespeare, I thought it was gonna be dead borin' . . .	
FRANK Then why did you go in the first place?	
RITA I wanted to find out. But listen, it wasn't borin', it was bleedin' great, honest, ogh, it done me in, it was fantastic. I'm gonna do an essay on it.	
FRANK (*smiling*) Come on, which one was it?	

3   Although Frank and Rita obviously come from different backgrounds, they clearly share a love of *Macbeth*. The language used by each character reflects their different backgrounds. Frank uses Standard English whereas Rita mostly uses regional dialect.

In pairs, find examples of the characters' different uses of language in this scene and note down them in a table like the one below. Rita's regional dialect and use of slang have been highlighted in bold. Use the examples on the next page as a guide.

Frank	Rita
I'm honoured that you chose me.	I know I shouldn't be here, it's **me** dinner hour, but listen, I've **gorra** tell someone, have y' got a few minutes, can **y'spare** . . .?

Section J: Comparison Activities

Year 7 Comparison Activities: Sections A–C

The activities in this section are designed to enhance your understanding of the way that the media influences our view of the world around us. The activities that you have completed in Sections A–C should have helped you explore the way that media devices in each script are used cleverly to appeal to a particular target audience. The following activities ask you to compare and contrast the scripts in Sections A–C. They will allow you to demonstrate and develop your ability to analyse the impact of the media across and within the genres of radio, TV and film.

1 Working in pairs, discuss and then decide who the target audience is for the scripts in Sections A–C. Copy and complete the table below and explain your decisions in column 3.

Remember that you can categorise an audience in the following ways:

- gender – male/female/both
- age group – young children, teenagers, adults, etc.
- lifestyle grouping – fans of sport, comedy, real-life drama, etc.

You should also consider the likely time when these media scripts would be aired or screened and the possibility that each may have more than one target audience.

Script	Target Audience	Explanation of why you think this
Radio Five Live Phone-in		
War of the Worlds		

Script	Target Audience	Explanation of why you think this
Kevin the Teenager		
Coronation Street		
Grange Hill		
House of Dracula		
Wallace and Gromit		
North by Northwest		

2   In the *Grange Hill*, *Coronation Street* and *Kevin the Teenager*
    scripts we are shown some of the problems that young people face
    in their teenage years. These range across the following:

    - parental pressure
    - developing your own identity
    - peer pressure
    - career choices
    - relationships with the opposite sex.

    In these scripts, Kevin, Mandy and Todd have to cope with one or
    more of these issues. Working independently, decide which of
    these teenage issues each character has to deal with. Using a
    table like the one on the next page, note down evidence of each
    issue from the scripts in column 3. Then explain how you feel the
    characters cope with each problem in column 4. One example has
    been done for you.

Character	Issues that the character deals with	Example from script which reveals this issue	How character copes with this teenage problem
Kevin	Relationship with parents	DAD Well it's fine for you to stay at Damon's, Kevin – why didn't you tell us the truth in the first place? KEVIN Ugh! Ugh! Ugh! Don't be so STUPID! you just DON'T UNDERSTAND DO YOU? HOW COULD I POSSIBLY TELL YOU THE TRUTH? YOU'RE MY PARENTS!	Kevin uses deceit and confrontation to try and gain an advantage over his parents.
Mandy			
Todd			

3   Imagine that you have been asked to host a radio phone-in based around the theme: 'Terrible Teens *or* Misunderstood Youths?' The discussion will centre on whether teenagers deserve our sympathy and understanding for the problems they face or whether society is too soft on them and they need greater discipline. It will be your job to make the phone-in balanced.

a) In groups of five, decide who will take on the following roles:

    - radio host (must be objective and balanced. See pages 15–21 for the way Fi Glover in the Radio Five Live Phone-in manages to stay objective whilst developing the views of others)
    - four listeners who phone in to give their views on the issue and to comment on their experiences. These four listeners are:
        - Kevin (*Kevin the Teenager*)
        - Mr Malachey (*Grange Hill*)
        - Todd Grimshaw (*Coronation Street*)
        - Eileen Grimshaw (*Coronation Street*).

b) Before you begin this role play, explore the likely thoughts of the phone-in contributors. Consider their opinions on teenagers and ensure that you will reflect their attitudes and use of language. For example, Kevin would not ring in saying 'If at all possible, I would like to engage in your most interesting topic of conversation . . . '. Your choice of language, tone, volume and way of interacting with the other callers should reflect your character's most likely thoughts on teenagers.

Use a table like the one on the next page to plan your responses. Remember that most of the discussion will be improvised, not scripted. This is a live broadcast, not a piece of rehearsed drama. Some entries have been completed for you.

Character	Likely views on teenagers	Personal experiences	Examples of the type of language they may use
Kevin			Ceeurgh! You lot are sooooo stuuupid. You DON'T understand nothing.
Mr Malachey	They are nothing but trouble. Have bad attitudes and are a nuisance who need much greater discipline.		
Todd	•		
Eileen		Her son, Todd, has just decided to give up all his studies and chances to go to university for a stupid teenage romance with that . . . Sarah Platt.	

4 All three screenplays in Section C provide excellent examples of how the script writers use stage directions carefully to develop the atmosphere of the scene. You will also notice the varied use of the following to add dramatic effect and appeal to their target audience:

- camera shots
- different character perspectives
- dramatic dialogue.

Although each script has its particular mood and plot, they all develop the sense of anticipation through these techniques. For this task you need to stretch your imagination by placing characters from one script into another. This should result in some humorous and exciting action. Working independently, choose one of the following scenarios and write a three-minute screenplay. Remember to use the film techniques discussed in Section C.

- Scenario 1: Wallace begins his day as a window cleaner and gets an unexpected knock at the window as he wakes Dracula from a deep but disturbed sleep.
- Scenario 2: Gromit replaces Vandamm in the scene from *North by Northwest*.

Remember to reflect the personalities, dialogue and actions of the characters, even though they are in unfamiliar roles.

5 The two radio scripts in Section A, *War of the Worlds* and *Radio Five Live Phone-in*, are vastly different in style, language, purpose and audience. In pairs, decide what you think the purpose of each script is. Is it to inform, shock, entertain, describe, amuse, discuss, persuade or . . . ?

6 The major difference between the two radio scripts is that one of them is fiction and the other is non-fiction. Copy the table on the next page and explain, in note form, how you can tell which script is fiction and which non-fiction. Use evidence from each script to support your ideas.

Script	Fiction or non-fiction?	Evidence from the text which reveals this
War of the Worlds		
Radio Five Live Phone-in		

7   Both radio scripts, though different in style and purpose, show how the language of radio broadcasting is often colloquial, immediate and does not always follow the rules of Standard English. Repetition, pauses and the speed of dialogue are all features of speech patterns that are common in live radio broadcasting. In pairs, find examples from both scripts which demonstrate these features and record them in a table like the one below.

Script	Colloquial language	Non-standard English	Repetition	Pauses (delayed speech)
War of the Worlds				
Radio Five Live Phone-in				

8   In *War of the Worlds*, *House of Dracula* and *North by Northwest*, the purpose of each script is to create tension and suspense. The writers have achieved this through the varied use of:

- sound
- camera shots
- dramatic use of language
- editing
- sense of realism.

In particular, the settings and characters are described powerfully to give the audience a sense of the atmosphere. For each script identify two examples of these descriptions of setting and character and record them in a table like the one below. Explain how effective they are in developing and maintaining tension for the audience. Some examples have been done for you.

Script	Settings described and effect	Characters described and effect
War of the Worlds	Wait a minute! Someone's crawling out of the hollow top. Someone or . . . something. I can see peering out of that black hole two luminous disks . . . are they eyes? It might be a face. It might be . . .	*The short dramatic sentence 'Wait a minute!' and the fact that it is an exclamation startles the audience into taking notice of the sight before it is revealed. Moreover, the use of the words 'someone, or something' adds to the mysterious atmosphere as it engages the audience with the speaker's sense of shock. Repetition is also used effectively 'It might be, it might be' to reinforce the sensation of awe and panic.*
House of Dracula	As it comes into a CLOSE SHOT and hovers toward the window, chittering softly while it looks o.s. with glittering eyes, the CAMERA PANS AWAY to another part of the room	*This opening description uses the sense of sound 'chittering' and personification 'glittering eyes' to develop the mood of mystery and the unknown. In particular, the*

Script	Settings described and effect	Characters described and effect
	creature's wings beat upon the wall beyond the bed inwhich lies a girl, Meliza Morelle. Her face, revealed in the moonlight streaming in through the window is beautiful. Reacting subconsciously to the o.s. SOUNDS of the bat's chittering, MELIZA stirs restively.	subconcious reactions of Meliza helps the audience to share the feeling of anticipation and anxiety.
North by Northwest		

Section J: Comparison Activities

Year 8 Comparison Activities: Sections D–F

The activities in this section are designed to enhance your understanding of the way that the media influences our view of the world around us. The activities that you have completed in Sections D–F should have helped you explore the way that media devices in each script are used cleverly to appeal to a particular target audience. The following activities ask you to compare and contrast the scripts in Sections D–F. They will allow you to demonstrate and develop your ability to analyse the impact of the media across and within the genres of radio, TV and film.

1   Through the three screenplays in Section F, the audience is shown different kinds of conflict that can be created within a family. Working independently, briefly describe the problems that the following characters face:

   - Billy (*Kes*)
   - Nazir (*East is East*)
   - Nathan (*The Full Monty*).

2   Each screenplay in Section F depicts certain realities of working-class life. These are presented to the audience through the descriptions of the settings and characters, as well as in dialogue. Working in pairs, find examples from the scripts that represent working-class culture to the audience. Some examples have been done for you.

Script	Description of settings	Description of character	Dialogue
Kes			MACDOWALL What's tha' gone over there for Casper frightened? What's up, don't you like company? They say your mother does – I've heard you've got more uncles than any kid in this city. *The other boys' reaction.* BILLY Shut your mouth.
East is East	*NAZIR backs away from George; he pulls off his turban and diadem and lets them fall to the ground, the tears leaving a long black line from the kohl on his eyes.*		
The Full Monty	*On the shop floor, MANDY is overseeing a line of women who are automatically snapping the arms of plastic dolls into their torsos.*		

3 In pairs, compare and contrast the struggles that Billy, Nazir and Nathan face in these scripts. Consider the following in your discussion:

- family conflicts
- relationship between the characters
- use of humour
- use of description.

4 In groups of four, plan a hot-seating exercise in which Billy, Nazir and Nathan are asked questions on their experiences in the scenes from the scripts.

a) First, write a list of questions that would help the audience to understand the feelings of the characters involved. Example questions might be:

For Billy – *How did you feel when Macdowall arrived?*
For Nazir – *Explain why you felt under so much pressure?*
For Nathan – *Why did you go behind your mum's back and use your savings?*

b) Then take it in turns to play Billy, Nazir or Nathan and answer the questions in character. The fourth member of your group will ask the questions.

5 Working independently, produce a short TV script based on one of these themes:

- caught between two cultures
- poverty
- bullying.

Remember to use these features of a film script:

- brief director's notes
- dialogue which reflects their speech in the existing script
- descriptions of the setting
- directions on characters' body language
- lighting
- sound effects
- camera angles (close up/long shot/ character perspective).

6   Thought-tracking is the drama technique where characters are asked
    to 'freeze' as one character 'unfreezes' to describe their innermost
    feelings about the other characters or themselves. It is an
    excellent device to help the audience identify with the characters.

    In groups of three, practise and perform the following dialogue
    extracts, using the thought-tracking technique. You will need to
    share the roles so that each of you acts in two scripts.

Script	Dialogue extracts for thought–tracking
Kes	MACDOWALL He's not your right brother, my mother says. They don't even call him Casper for a start.
	BILLY Course he's my brother! We live in the same house, don't we?
	MACDOWALL And he don't look a bit like thee, he's twice as big for a start, you're nowt like brothers.
	BILLY runs at him, shouting that he's going to tell Jud what MacDowall's said.
	MACDOWALL pushes Billy off with his foot, and as BILLY comes back he punches him hard which sends him flying back on a heap.
	MACDOWALL Get away, you little squirt, before I spit on you and drown you.
East is East	The BRIDE's FAMILY is now looking over, concerned at the delay. The MULLAH is looking at George questioningly. GEORGE goes towards Nazir, NAZIR backs away from George; he pulls off his turban and diadem and lets them fall to the ground, the tears leaving a long black line from the kohl on his eyes.
	GEORGE Sit down, no do this.
	NAZIR I'm sorry, Dad.
	GEORGE grabs Nazir and slaps him.

Script	Dialogue extracts for thought–tracking
The Full Monty	GAZ Well, when you're eighteen you can walk in here and get it yourself, can't you?
	NATHAN You said you'd get it back.
	GAZ (reasoning) I know, but you don't want to listen to what I say.
	NATHAN You said so. I believe you.
	GAZ You do?
	NATHAN Yes.
	GAZ Blimey, Nath.

7   In the TV scripts in Section E, much of the comic effect is generated through the comic devices shown in the table.

   a) Working in pairs, compare the way that humour is created by completing a table like the one below. Some examples have been done for you.

Comic devices	Only Fools and Horses	A Bit of Fry and Laurie	Blackadder Goes Forth
Mocking stereotypes		HUGH I mean it's not all fell-walking and climbing boots. STEPHEN No. Right. HUGH You should see some of the traffic we get in Thirsk and Harrogate. STEPHEN Oh.	

Comic devices	Only Fools and Horses	A Bit of Fry and Laurie	Blackadder Goes Forth
		HUGH And the pollution in Leeds can rival anything you've got down south, we like to think.	
Use of puns and wordplay			
Misinter-pretation			
Mocking serious issues			MELCHETT So, it's maximum security, is that clear? BLACKADDER Quite so sir, only myself and the rest of the English-speaking world is to know.

Comic devices	Only Fools and Horses	A Bit of Fry and Laurie	Blackadder Goes Forth
One-liners	DEL And the place we stayed at – cor, dear – the room was never swept, the food was diabolical, and the sheets, they weren't changed from one week to the next. RODNEY You should have gone self-catering. DEL We did.		

b) Working independently, use the ideas recorded in the table above to write a detailed comparison of the way humour is created in *Only Fools and Horses* and *A Bit of Fry and Laurie* and *Blackadder Goes Forth*.

8 Script writers choose to explore the issue of stereotyping in different ways. Some write seriously to show the pain caused by stereotypes, whereas others use humour in their writing as a means to expose them. In pairs, compare and contrast the way that stereotypes are presented to the audience in the following scripts:

- *East is East* (arranged marriages/racial stereotypes and prejudice)
- *The Full Monty* (working-class stereotypes)
- *A Bit of Fry and Laurie* (northerner and southerner)
- *Only Fools and Horses* (eastender, wide-boy stereotypes).

In your analysis focus on:

- settings
- character names
- non-standard English (e.g. slang and dialect).

9   Although the radio scripts in Section D are both examples of live entertainment, they differ greatly in their style, purpose and target audience. Explain what is meant by these terms and provide examples to justify your viewpoint.

10 In pairs, find examples of how the *Live Football Commentary* and the *Live Interview with Will Smith* each use metaphors to entertain their target audiences.

11 Both radio scripts use informal, colloquial, non-standard English to create the sense of immediacy needed for a live broadcast. Working in pairs, rewrite parts of the original dialogue as formal, standard English, in a table like the one below. Make sure that you use correct style and punctuation where required. The first example has been done for you.

Script	Original dialogue	Standard English
Live Football Commentary	SCHMEICHEL Yeah, well, I don't want to say anything, I'll let you two say whatever – GREEN Well, it's just a ridiculous decision . . . absolutely laughable . . . BUTCHER A farce, absolute farce! GREEN Hah!	SCHMEICHEL Yes, I most certainly agree. I would rather not say anything on the matter. I believe it would be best if I leave you two to describe your own thoughts on the matter.

Script	Original dialogue	Standard English
Live Interview with Will Smith	WILL Yeah. It was a little tight when I first put it on, as I was coming off of Ali and I was a little bigger than when I made the last film. But no, it felt good, man, getting back. It's like, you know, family coming back together, you know – the director, and the co-stars. When you're making a sequel it's like coming back together more than when you start a film, it's really you're getting to know people and it's a slow start and all that. We really kind of hit the ground running.	

12 All the scripts in Sections D–F have a particular purpose. Their success depends on whether the writer or presenter is able to adjust the style of delivery to meet the needs of their particular target audience. Working in pairs, use the list below to decide on the different purposes of each script. Write these as shown in the table on the next page. The first one has been done for you.

Possible purposes:

- to inform
- to explain
- to promote
- to describe
- to excite

- to entertain
- to shock
- to educate (raise awareness of a particular issue).

Script	Explanation of purpose
Live Interview with Will Smith	*To inform the listeners of Will Smith's new film* *To promote and market the film to the public.* *To entertain the audience through the clever use of language, humour and word play.*
Live Football Commentary	
Only Fools and Horses	
Blackadder Goes Forth	
A Bit of Fry and Laurie	
Kes	
East is East	
The Full Monty	

Section J: Comparison Activities

Year 9 Comparison Activities: Sections G–I

The activities in this section are designed to enhance your understanding of the way that the media influences our view of the world around us. The activities that you have completed in Sections G–I should have helped you explore the way that media devices in each script are used cleverly to appeal to a particular target audience. The following activities ask you to compare and contrast the scripts in Sections D–F. They will allow you to demonstrate and develop your ability to analyse the impact of the media across and within the genres of radio, TV and film.

1   Many of the characters in Sections G–I find themselves in challenging and emotionally-charged situations. The writers of these scripts invite the audience to join these characters on their emotional roller coasters.

Using a table like the one below, describe the situation in which each of the characters finds themselves.

Character	Challenging situation
Toby Farnham	
Arthur Dent	
Tony	
Jim	
Basil	
Hortense	
Young Paul	
Rita	

2 The level of seriousness depends on the particular circumstances of the character's situation. In some scripts, the writer clearly does not want the audience to take the action too seriously and therefore they laugh at the ridiculous situation rather than empathise.

a) In pairs, rank the character's circumstances by level of seriousness (least serious = 1, most serious = 8).

1	Rita – She has to get back to work to finish a perm. Doesn't know what to wear for dinner party.
2	
3	
4	
5	
6	
7	
8	Hortense – After recently dealing with the death of her adoptive mother, Hortense visits the adoption agency to find out who her real mum is.

b) Through pair discussion, compare the way these characters deal with their difficult situation. For example, through anger, surprise, sarcasm, tears, restrained emotion, humour, panic, etc.

3 The settings of the scripts in Sections G–I contribute greatly to the dramatic effect on the audience.

a) Copy and complete the table below, briefly describing each· setting in your own words. Some examples have been done for you.

Script	Settings	Brief description
FX	Car Road Church Studio	
The Hitchhiker's Guide to the Galaxy		
Men Behaving Badly		
The Royle Family		
Fawlty Towers	Fawlty Towers hotel	
Secrets and Lies		
Educating Rita		
Fever Pitch	House Car Chip shop Football stadium	

b) Compare the way that the settings help to create a particular mood and atmosphere in each of these scripts.

4 Using the three screenplay extracts in Section I, compare in writing how the theme of education is presented to the audience? Consider the following:

- what the characters hope to learn
- what they may be afraid to learn
- how they feel as a result of the educational experience.

Remember to use some of the connectives in the list below in your piece of comparative writing:

Useful connectives
• **To add a point:** in addition, furthermore, moreover, another point is, some people argue that . . .
• **To contradict an argument:** although, but, even, though, however, in contrast, in spite of, instead, nevertheless, nonetheless, on the contrary, on one hand . . . on the other hand, yet
• **To show cause and effect:** accordingly, as a result, because, consequently, for this purpose, hence, so, then, therefore, thereupon, thus, to this end
• **To summarise a point or conclude:** in short, on the whole, therefore, to summarise accordingly, as a result, because, consequently, for this purpose, hence, so, then, therefore, thus, to this end

5   In the TV scripts in Section H, some of the characters find
     themselves in situations which are beyond their control. Jim needs
     to keep his daughter calm as she is about to give birth soon; Basil
     has to react to an awkward customer; Tony will need to explain
     why there is a cocktail drink splattered around Deborah's
     underwear drawer and bedspread.

     In groups of three, practise and perform the following extracts
     from the TV scripts, using thought-tracking. Thought-tracking is
     the drama technique where characters are asked to 'freeze' and
     one character 'unfreezes' to describe their innermost feelings.
     Decide which character at which moment has the most comic
     tension for thought-tracking. Share the roles so that each of you
     acts in two scripts.

Script	Extracts from the script	Thought –tracking
Fawlty Towers	RONALD ... God, you're dumb.	
	MRS HEATH Oh, now ...	
	BASIL (*controlling himself*) Is there something we can get you instead sonny?	
	RONALD I'd like some bread and salad cream.	
	BASIL ... To eat? Well ... (*Pointing*) there's the bread, and there's the mayonnaise.	
	RONALD I said salad cream, stupid.	

Script	Extracts from the script	Thought –tracking
Men Behaving Badly	Tony turns to another page at the end of the diary. He reaches for his cocktail, which is on the chest of drawers. DEBORAH'S VOICE-OVER Tony behaved like a complete idiot today – In surprise he knocks the full glass into the open knicker drawer. TONY Aaarrghh! He jumps about, wondering what to do. In panic, he removes the drawer and empties it out on the pastel duvet, which is instantly spattered with stains. Tony stands there turning this way and that in panic.	
The Royle Family	DENISE Come in, Dad. Come in. JIM It's not too messy is it? DENISE No. Come in. Jim goes in. Denise is sitting on the edge of the bath, doubled over. Jim puts the toilet seat down and sits on it, comforting his sobbing daughter.	

6 Stereotypes are used effectively in the three TV scripts to communicate a particular message to the audience whilst making them humorous. Identify the stereotypes which are presented in *The Royle Family, Men Behaving Badly, Fever Pitch* and *Educating Rita,* and explain the message that is being conveyed by each.

7 In groups of three, improvise a conversation between Gary (*Men Behaving Badly*), Jim (*The Royle Family*) and Paul (*Fever Pitch*) about whether family or football should come first.

You must accurately reflect their personalities and be convincing in your tone of voice, body language and speech.

8 The events depicted in the scripts in Sections G–I range across realism and fantasy. Decide which scripts present life in a realistic way and which in a fantastical way. Note down your decisions in a table like the one below. Then explain, giving details of character, setting and dialogue, how each creates a sense of fantasy or realism. Use the examples to guide you.

Script	Realism, fantasy or a mix of both	Explanation to support this view
FX	fantasy	Although the beginning seems very real, the final over-exaggerated language of the horror movie genre mocks the clichés of mystery writing. Therefore the audience is not expected to take this extract seriously, and instead joins in the fantasy.
The Hitchhiker's Guide to the Galaxy		
Secrets and Lies		

Script	Realism, fantasy or a mix of both	Explanation to support this view
The Royle Family	both realism and fantasy	The setting and dialogue is a realistic picture of northern working-class culture, although the humour is so elaborate and exaggerated at times that the audience is not expected to take the action too seriously. We have every confidence the baby will be fine.
Men Behaving Badly		
Fawlty Towers		
Educating Rita		
Fever Pitch		

Chart Relating Activities to Framework Objectives for Key Stage 3

Chapter	Year Group	Media	Extract	Word Level (WL)	Sentence Level (SL)	Text Level Reading (TLR)	Text Level Writing (TLW)	Speaking and Listening (S&L)
A1	7	Radio	War of the Worlds, pp1–14		S&L5 (Activity 1); S&L10 (Activity 2); S&L9 (Activity 3)		TLW2 (Activity 1)	
A2	7	Radio	Radio Five Live Phone-in, pp15–24		SL12, 13f, 15 (Activity 3)	TLR1, 4, 9 (Activity 2)	TLW1, 15, 19 (Activity 1); TLW2, 10 (Activity 2); TLW12, 18 (Activity 3)	
B1	7	TV	Kevin The Teenager, pp25–33		SL16 (Activity 1); SL12 (Activity 4)	TLR4 (Activity 1); TLR18 (Activity 2)	TLW 6 (Activity 1); TLW1 (Activity 4, 5)	S&L 16, 17 (Activity 3) S&L 12, 14 (Activity 4)
B2	7	TV	Coronation Street, pp34–39			TLR4, 8 (Activity 1); TLR14 (Activity 2)	TLW2 (Activity 1,2); TLW6 (Activity 3)	S&L17 (Activity 2); S&L15, 16 (Activity 3)
B3	7	TV	Grange Hill, pp40–47				TLW17 (Activity 4)	S&L11, 12, 13, 15, 16 (Activity 1); S&L17, 19 (Activity 2)
C1	7	Film	Dracula, pp48–58			TLR 6 (Activity 1); TLR10, 11 (Activity 1, 2)	TLW2 (Activity 1,2); TLW6 (Activity 3,4); TLW9 (Activity 3, 5); TLW14 (Activity 3)	S&L12 (Activity 2)
C2	7	Film	Wallace and Gromit, pp59–68			TLR 10, 11 (Activity 1) TLR8 (Activity 2) TLR3 (Activity 3);	TLW2 (Activity 1); TLW6 (Activity 2); TLW9 (Activity 4,5);	S&L 12 (Activity 3); S&L 16 (Activity 5)
C3	7	Film	North by Northwest, pp69–77			TLR3, 9 (Activity 1)	TLW3 (Activity 1); TLW2, 5, 6 (Activity 2)	S&L 9, 12, 14, 16 (Activity 3)
D1	8	Radio	Live Football Commentary, pp78–85	WL12 (Activity 2)		TLR3, 9 (Activity 1, 3); TLR4 (Activity 1)	TLW12 (Activity 2)	
D2	8	Radio	Live Interview with Will Smith, pp86–91	WL11 (Activity 2)		TLR3 (Activity 1)	TLW10 (Activity 3)	S&L10 (Activity 2, 3) S&L4, 11, 12 (Activity 3)

E1	8	TV	Only Fools and Horses, pp92–98	W19 (Activity 1)	SL9 (Activity 1)	TLR3 (Activity 1)	TLW1, 10 (Activity 1)	S&L1, 2, 8, 9, 11, 15, 16 (Activity 1)
E2	8	TV	A Bit of Fry and Laurie, pp99–105	WL13 (Activity 1)		TLR3, 7 (Activity 1)	TLW7 (Activity 3)	S&L7, 10, 11, 12 (Activity 2) S&L16 (Activity 3)
E3	8	TV	Blackadder Goes Forth, pp106–115	WL19, 13 (Activity 1)		TLR3, 5, 7 (Activity 1)	TLW1, 7 (Activity 2)	S&L2, 5 (Activity 2); S&L8, 11, 14, 15 (Activity 2)
F1	8	Film	Kes, pp116–122		SL4, 9 (Activity 3)	TLR1, 3 (Activity 1) TLR5 (Activity 1, 2)	TLW5, 8 (Activity 2)	S&L1, 5, 11, 12 (Activity 2)
F2	8	Film	The Full Monty, pp123–128	WL12 (Activity 1)	SL11 (Activity 1); SL12 (Activity 2)	TLR3 (Activity 1)		S&L 14, 16 (Activity 3)
F3	8	Film	East is East, pp129–135		SL9 (Activity 4)	TLR4, 7 (Activity 1) TLR1, 3, (Activity 2) TLR5 (Activity 2, 3)	TLW 3 (Activity 2)	S&L2, 3, 11 (Activity 1); S&L9, 12, 14, 15, 16 (Activity 4)
G1	9	Radio	The Hitchhiker's Guide to the Galaxy, pp136–143		SL3, 9 (Activity 1)	TLR2 (Activity 1)	TLW10 (Activity 1); TLW6, 7 (Activity 2, 3)	S&L10 (Activity 2)
G2	9	Radio	F/X, pp144–149			TLR1 (Activity 1)	TLW2 (Activity 1); TLW5, 6 (Activity 2)	S&L4, 5, 12, 14 (Activity 3)
H1	9	TV	The Royle Family, pp150–157				TLW4, 7 (Activity 1)	S&L1, 4, 5, 9, 10, 11, 12, 15 (Activity 1)
H2	9	TV	Men Behaving Badly, pp158–165			TLR12 (Activity 1) TLR7 (Activity 1, 2, 3); TLR6 (Activity 2, 3)		S&L 10, 12, 14 (Activity 2, 3)
H3	9	TV	Fawlty Towers, pp166–172		SL4 (Activity 1); SL9 (Activity 3)	TLR1 (Activity 1)	TLW7 (Activity 1); TLW13 (Activity 3)	S&L12, 14 (Activity 2)
I1	9	Film	Fever Pitch, pp173–184		SL4 (Activity 1)	TLR1, 2 (Activity 1)	TLW1, 4, 7 (Activity 3)	S&L3, 5, 7, 9 (Activity 2)
I2	9	Film	Secrets and Lies, pp185–193	SL1, 3 (Activity 1)	TLR1 (Activity 1, 2);	TIW1, 6, 11 (Activity 1); TLR 3 (Activity 1); TLR2 (Activity 2)	S&L5, 9, 10 (Activity 3); TLW9 (Activity 1, 3); TLW4, 12, 15, 16 (Activity 3)	
I3	9	Film	Educating Rita, pp194–203	WL7 (Activity 1)		TLR1 (Activity 1)	TLW 17 (Activity 1); TLW1, 5 (Activity 2)	S&L2, 9 (Activity 3)
J			Comparisons pp204–230					

Glossary

A-list	Hottest celebrities of the moment
anthropologists	People who study humans
au naturel	Naked
BEAT	A second of silence in a film, used to create an effect
candelabrum	An ornamental holder with branches in which candles are supported
chavvies	Children
close shot	A scene showing items/characters close to the camera
closeup	A scene showing items/character very close to the camera
detritus	Debris
demented	Crazy
dissolve out	Scene dissolves into blackness
eject	Throw out
ext.	External scene
fade in	The scene fades in from blackness
fervently	Enthusiastically
full shot	A scene showing a wide area
FX	Special effects
Henry Kissinger	US Secretary of State 1973–77 and Nobel Peace Prize winner
innuendoes	An indirect comment, such as a hint
insert	To put something in
int.	Internal scene
intercut	Several camera angles shown one after another
infidelity	Unfaithfulness
Kenneth Wolstenholme	Legendary football commentator
khazi	Toilet
Maginot Line	A defense built between 1929 and 1940 to protect France from Germany

masonry	Stonework
med. shot	A scene showing items/characters relatively close to the camera
moving shot	A scene in which the camera moves
off mike	Not spoken directly into microphone
o.s	Off screen
OOV	Out of vision
pea souper	Thick fog
panning up	Camera moves upwards
pirate radio station	Illegal radio station
point-blank	Extremely close range
popular culture	Trends, fashions and opinions that are important in current society
pouffe	A large thick cushion, used as a seat or footstool.
POV	Point of view
Pulitzer Prize	An American award for excellence in journalism, music, literature or drama
Robert Carrier	Famous French chef
sarky	Sarcastic
sequences	The order in which one or more things follow each other
shrewd	Wise
stop-frame animation	Animation that creates movement by moving a character/object in tiny amounts and photographing each movement.
strident	Loud
synergy	Merging of interests
time-slot	The time a programme is on TV
top-hole	Excellent
tracks in	The camera moves in closer to an item/character
two shot	A scene in which two people are shown on camera at the same time
voice-over	A voice that is heard by the audience, but the character is not seen.
watershed	A time after which adult television can be broadcast; or a dividing point